Woman of the Promise

Shirley Ballantine

Dedication

To my beautiful daughters, Katrina Mary and
Michelle Elizabeth.

My thanks to my husband Jim for his support, and to
my son-in-law Stephen for his technical help, both of
which are deeply appreciated.

Chapter 1

For a long time he had been watching her. Day after day his eyes would follow her as she roamed in the exquisite garden, touching delicate flowers with dainty fingers, or reaching up to pick luscious fruit from laden trees, her body lithe and graceful, a smile of happiness playing about her soft lips.

"Soon, soon, it must be soon," he whispered to himself.

He kept low, out of sight, his long sinuous body slithering along the grass, in and out through the trees. He felt uncomfortable in a place of such perfection, but he must follow the woman, watch her, wait for his chance.

She was beautiful, this woman: perfect in form, lovely in face, delightful, charming, full of life and love and laughter. And innocence. Above all else innocence.

He had seen her with the man. He had watched them strolling together in the garden hand in hand, or laughing companionably as they sat under the shade of a tree.

They were in such perfect accord with one another, yet each possessed an independence of spirit which allowed them to follow their own inclinations at will. The man enjoyed spending time with the animals, revelling in their beauty and variety, their speed and agility. The woman loved to smell the perfume of the flowers, or wander among the trees listening to the melodious sound of bird-song. Often they sauntered by the river together, or swam in its sparkling waters, the joyous sound of their laughter ringing in the clear air.

"I need to get her alone," he muttered, with an evil glint in his eye.

He raised himself up to look around. As far as the eye could see all was beauty and order. Trees and flowers, rivers and mountains, birds and animals; all were in harmony with each other and with the humans.

"All that will change!" he leered maliciously.

He would have to be subtle, but that would not be difficult. He had complete confidence in his ability. He would win. She would lose. She who had all that heart could desire would lose everything. And nothing would ever be the same again.

"I will destroy her," he hissed, venom in his tongue.

His eyes gleamed with malevolence as they followed the woman. She had left the man sitting by the river and had wandered off on her own as she was wont to do. Soon she reached a little grove of fruit trees from where the silvery gleam of the river could still just be seen in the distance. She roved around, enjoying the delights of sight and smell, touch and taste in the bountiful orchard. Now was his chance! She was alone, and that she was here in this secluded grove would suit his purpose well.

He approached her, pulling himself up to his greatest height. He would speak to her. He would use all the guile and treachery of which he was capable. He would not fail!

He moved nearer. First he would dazzle her with his charm, then he would beguile her. Closer he crept, his movements graceful, his agile body silently swaying and gyrating.

She had caught sight of him. He could see her eyes widen slightly in surprise, then her lips curved in a smile of pleasure. He danced for her and she laughed aloud and clapped her hands. Such happiness, such perfection, such innocence! He would strike now! He would ruin her!

The woman selected a piece of fruit and seated herself ready to eat. It was his cue.

"Did God really say, 'You must not eat from any tree in the garden'?" he insinuated cunningly.

Again the woman's eyes widened.

"We may eat fruit from the trees in the garden, but God did say, 'You must not eat fruit from the tree that is in the middle of the garden', and you must not touch it," she added, "'or you will die.'"

He could see that he had made her think, sown a small seed of doubt in her mind. He pressed his advantage.

"You will not surely die," he told her, his manner confidential and reassuring. "For God knows that when you eat of it your eyes will be opened, and you will be like God, knowing good and evil."

The woman had known only good. What would it be like to know everything, like God? She hesitated, thinking. The fruit of this tree would bring a new knowledge, the clever, handsome creature said.

She arose and walked over to where the tree was growing, not far away. Now that she looked at it, this tree was magnificent in its beauty, it bore excellent fruit which she longed to taste, and it would give her infinite wisdom. Three good reasons! She could have all this, and no harm would come to her. Why hesitate any longer?

She reached out her hand and plucked a piece of fruit from the tree. Turning it over in her hands she admired the subtle colouring and soft bloom of its velvety skin. Holding it up to her face she caught a whiff of its delectable aroma. She was about to taste it when she suddenly had a thought. Turning back she picked another piece.

"We will enjoy it together," she smiled to herself.

Running, fleet of foot, calling his name, she soon came upon the man where he was sitting on the river bank watching the fish dart through the water.

The serpent watched her go. Heartlessly he laughed.

"Mission accomplished!" he sneered as he glided away.

He would follow and view the downfall from a better vantage point. Then, for a time, he would vanish like an angel of light.

Chapter 2

A deep stillness had descended upon the garden. It was as if all nature had been stunned into silence. Surpassing the stillness in its intensity was the sorrow that filled the heart of a woman, once so pure and innocent, now so blemished and guilty.

Under the leafy canopy of the densest trees in the wood she lay on the ground writhing in anguish and shame. No sunlight filtered through the foliage, nor did she wish any. She could not bear that blazing light to shine on her. She was naked and she knew it. Worse even than that, her soul was bare before that scorching light, exposed to the burning fire of God's holiness.

Pangs of remorse rolled over her like waves on the sand, ever ebbing and flowing. Pain throbbed in her heart.

"What have I done, oh what have I done?" she moaned, tears flowing down her beautiful face.

Grief and despair gripped her soul. She longed, oh how she longed to turn back time, to be what she had once been, to know only good. How wise and loving God had been to withhold the knowledge of evil. If only she had trusted Him! If only she had been content to live as He had wanted her to live, pure and free!

Why had she listened to that hateful creature? He lied to her. He dared to contradict God, and she had believed him. He had beguiled her.

Even as her mind struggled with these thoughts, she knew deep in her heart that pride had made her desire the knowledge that the serpent offered her. For the moment she had forgotten about God and His commandment with the promise of this superior wisdom that the creature assured her she could have without coming to any harm herself.

"But he lied, he deliberately lied. I know that now," she wept.

He had set a trap for her and she had fallen into it. She had believed his word instead of God's. How wrong she had been!

"Oh, if only I had not listened to him!" she groaned.

But it was too late to wish that now. What was done was done. There was no turning back.

She sat up slowly and shivered. Soon it would be time to meet with God in the cool of the day. How would she face Him? What would she say to Him?

"I must go and find Adam," she sobbed.

Grief filled her mind anew at the thought of her husband. Dear Adam! She had caused him to disobey God. She had given him the fruit and he had eaten it.

He was not far away. Hiding under the trees as she herself had done, he was sitting with head bowed, eyes downcast. She seated herself beside him but he did not look at her. Instantly she sensed a barrier between them. They needed to talk but neither of them knew what to say. Gone was the happy companionship, the trust, perhaps even the love, she thought. Did he blame her for what had happened? She turned away, a sob catching in her throat.

Silently she arose and left him sitting there. They needed to prepare for the meeting with God, and a covering was necessary. She looked around to find something suitable, and finally selected some fig leaves which she managed to join together. It was inadequate but it would have to do. Bringing enough for Adam she returned to him.

He was as she had left him, deep in his own thoughts, his own guilt, his own desolation. Tears rolled down the woman's lovely face once more. Was there no hope for them?

In silent despair she sat down beside Adam until the last rays of the sun began to fade as it sank slowly in the west. Already they could hear God walking in the garden, and in their fear and dread shrank deeper into the shadows of the trees.

Clad in the garments of their own making they remained hidden there, waiting for the call which they knew would surely come. When it did they would have to answer. They knew it was useless to try to hide from God, and He would demand an account of themselves.

Suddenly God's voice rang out through the stillness.

"Where are you?"

Adam, stirred to speech at last, replied reluctantly, fearfully.

"I heard You walking in the garden, and I was afraid because I was naked, so I hid."

"Who told you that you were naked?" demanded God. "Have you eaten from the tree of which I commanded you not to eat?"

Adam cleared his throat and spoke again in a hoarse, low voice.

"The woman You put here with me–she gave me some fruit from the tree, and I ate it."

The woman caught her breath sharply. So he did blame her! Her mind was reeling with hurt and humiliation and fear. She longed to get away somewhere by herself, but God was speaking to her now and He required an answer.

"What is this you have done?" He asked.

Her mouth was dry and her heart was pounding, but she knew she must answer.

"The ... the serpent beguiled me and I ate," she stammered.

As she spoke she suddenly caught sight of the loathsome creature peering through the trees, his evil eyes gleaming with self-satisfaction as he surveyed the scene. No doubt he had come back to gloat over his success, she thought wearily.

The Lord God turned to the serpent and His voice thundered through the garden.

"Because you have done this," He declared, "Cursed are you above all the livestock and all the wild animals! You will crawl on your belly and you will eat dust all the days of your life. And I will put enmity between you and the woman, and between your offspring and hers; he will crush your head, and you will strike his heel."

Even in her distress the woman noticed that God did not ask the serpent why he had done this, as He had asked her and Adam. Clearly God knew why. And in meting out punishment to the serpent God had given her a ray of hope! Her heart skipped a beat as she heard how she herself was to be involved in it. Her offspring would crush his head, even though in doing so he himself would be wounded. Joy and sorrow simultaneously pierced her heart.

Turning away from the serpent God spoke again to the woman.

"I will greatly increase your pains in childbearing," He said. "With pain you will give birth to children. Your desire will be for your husband, and he will rule over you."

The woman bowed her head. What God said hurt deeply, but she knew she was guilty before Him.

But God was not finished yet. Finally He spoke to Adam.

"Because you listened to your wife, and ate from the tree about which I commanded you, 'You must not eat of it', "Cursed is the ground because of you; through painful toil you will eat of it all the days of your life. It will produce thorns and thistles for you, and you will eat the plants of the field. By the sweat of your brow you will eat your food until you return to the ground, since from it you were taken; for dust you are and to dust you will return."

The man and the woman stood aghast and trembling. Their punishments were terrible, yet they were no more than they deserved. In the midst of their horror they acknowledged that. God had been just. He was holy and pure; they were now but sinful creatures, subject to sorrow and hardship, and deprived of the immortality for which they were created. Their bodies would eventually experience physical death, for they were but dust and they would return to that state.

Sobs wracked the woman's frame as she realised the full significance of all that God had said. She had lost everything, everything, and she only had herself to blame.

Then at the point of her greatest need she felt Adam's arm around her as he gently drew her head down on his shoulder. To feel his love and sympathy only induced more tears, for she felt so undeserving, but she could see that God's pronouncement had forced him to accept responsibility for his own actions, and he was willing to forgive her. How it gladdened her heart in the midst of all her agony!

Adam was whispering gentle words.

"I have found a name for you at last," he said. "I will call you Eve because you will become a life-giver, the giver of life to our son who will one day vanquish the serpent. God has given His word, and we will never doubt it again."

The woman sighed. Why, oh why, had she ever doubted it in the first place? But Adam was right. They would never doubt it again. They were both deeply sorry for what they had done, and they would suffer the con-sequences of their actions, but God in His mercy had not left them without hope. The serpent's doom was sealed for God had spoken it.

Slowly they became aware that God, in spite of what they had done, still loved them and would always provide for them, even though the provision would bring both bane and blessing.

They watched with deep sadness as God took two of the animals He had created and made them clothes with the skins. They realised it was because of their sin that the blood of these lovely creatures had to be shed, and it must have hurt God deeply to do it, but there was no other way He could provide a covering for them. It was one of the saddest things in that saddest of all days.

Then, under the warmth and protection of their new covering they had to leave the beautiful garden where they had known so much happiness.

As she looked back wistfully, Eve realised it now belonged to the past. Never again would she know the perfect peace and joy she had known there. Never again would she eat freely of the fruit or wander at will among the flowers. From henceforth Adam would have to toil and sweat to produce food, and she would bear children in pain. Their lot would be as God decreed, toil and suffering.

But there was hope! She was forgiven, she was covered, and she had a promise. God had given His promise that one day her offspring would crush the serpent. That was a day worth living for!

Chapter 3

Eve had never thought it possible to feel joy and happiness again, but today was a day of rejoicing. She held her new-born son in her arms, and the sweetness of motherhood warmed her heart once more as the morning sun warms the earth.

Instantly her mind turned back to God's promise.

"Her offspring will crush your head."

The evil eyes, the poisonous tongue, the clever brain would be crushed, to deceive and beguile no longer. His power would be broken.

She and Adam had long since come to understand that the serpent who had deceived them in the garden was more than just one of the animals God had created. He had used the serpent's body, but in reality he was an evil being of great power whose aim was to corrupt the whole human race, and he had well-nigh succeeded in doing so. If God had not been merciful and promised to destroy the serpent, there would be no hope. But God in His infinite wisdom could see what the Evil One had tried to do , and He would not let him get away with it.

"Hence His promise," said Eve with satisfaction.

The woman's offspring would crush the serpent.

Often Eve had wondered why God had said, "the offspring of the woman". Why had He not said "the offspring of the man and the woman"? Perhaps, in His kindness He had wanted to encourage her, for she had been the one to lead them both into sin against Him. Perhaps there was another reason. Perhaps she would never know.

Eve sighed. She just had to hold on to that promise in faith, although it would not be easy in view of what had already happened. She had known deep disappointment and sorrow through her first two sons. This time though, it was different. This time God had given her the assurance that she so desperately needed. This child was the one who would lead to the fulfilment of God's plan to defeat the serpent.

"I will call him Seth," she said, "For God has appointed me another child in place of Abel whom Cain killed."

Her eyes filled with tears, and she felt that old familiar pain at the thought of the boys she had brought into the world. Full of hope and promise, she had given birth to Cain, her first-born. She remembered the thrill of knowing motherhood for the first time. There had been pain and distress, but when she held her baby in her arms it had been worth it all. The anguish had vanished like darkness disappearing at the sun's rising. In her happiness she cried out joyously,

"God has given me a man-child!".

She called him simply Cain because she had acquired him from the Lord.

Later when she had a second son, she thought it fitting to remember that he was of the earth, a transitory being, here for a season but subject to physical death. She named him Abel.

"How could I have known that beautiful, wonderful day of his birth, that his life would be so short, so fleeting," she reflected sadly.

Looking back now the name seemed even more appropriate.

Her heart filled with pain as she relived the childhood and manhood of the boys. She could see herself in Cain; the pride and the wilfulness, thinking he could do it all by himself. Abel was different; more sensitive, more thoughtful, more spiritual. As they grew into manhood she could see that Abel was more likely to be the child of the promise, the one who would crush the Evil One. It was clear that Cain had no interest in spiritual matters. He did not care to do battle with the serpent.

"Abel could have been the one," wept Eve, "but it was not to be."

As they brought their offering to God, just as she and Adam had taught them to do, Abel was the one who understood. He knew there was only one way to atone for his sinfulness. It was the way God had shown to Adam and herself when He clothed them with the skins of animals. Blood had to be shed, and Abel did not hesitate to offer his finest lambs. Cain in his pride and self-righteousness brought the fruit of the ground upon which he had bestowed his labour, but it was of no avail. God would not have it and told Cain so. God had given him every opportunity, but sadly Cain would not repent, and in his jealous anger committed murder against his brother.

Eve's heart ached with the memory of it. She had lost three children in one day, for Cain had gone, taking with him her lovely daughter as his wife, and she knew she would never see them again.

As they laid Abel's body in the ground the sorrow seemed unbearable, all the more so because she knew that she herself had been the means of bringing it all about. She and Adam had been responsible for bringing the curse of sin on human nature, and everyone born into the world was born under this curse, with a sinful nature as their inheritance. Only through God's mercy would they be forgiven.

She looked down at her new-born baby again.

"He looks so pure and perfect and innocent," she whispered, "but he is not."

She knew that never would a human being be born perfect and pure. Those qualities belonged only to God, and humans were totally dependent on Him for mercy and forgiveness.

"How kind and merciful He has been to me," she thought.

He had given her offspring as He had promised, thus giving her hope. And with the pain of childbirth came the blessing, something only a woman could know–the joy of motherhood. And although she could no longer act independently of Adam, that too proved to be a blessing. As head of the family it was Adam's responsibility to care for her and for their children.

Away back in the beginning God had said, "A man will be united to his wife, and they will become one flesh."

This was what God intended when He made her from a rib taken from Adam's side. He did not make her from Adam's head to be superior to him, nor from his feet to be inferior to him, but from his side, close to his heart, to be equal to him and loved by him. They were a partnership, each having qualities which complemented the other's. They loved each other and were one in their desire to live for the benefit of the other and for their offspring.

"It was different in our old life in the garden," Eve recalled. "We were as God intended us to be, sinless and innocent."

There had been no need for a headship then because all was order and perfection. Now, since the old order had gone and nothing was perfect any more, a head was needed in the partnership, and it was given to the husband, who was to rule as graciously and benignly as the sun ruled over the day and the moon over the night. Her husband was to be there by her side to help and advise.

"If he had been there by my side that fateful day in the garden would everything have been different?" she wondered.

She had been alone then without guidance or support, as the Evil One had planned it no doubt, and she had fallen.

Eve sighed and stirred from her reverie. She was thankful for Adam's love and strength. Truly what a good husband he was, and what a wise and wonderful God was hers, showing His love and care and provision for her in every way!

The baby whimpered and Eve lifted him gently and held him close.

"What a precious little soul!" she whispered.

God had given her fresh hope in sending her this son. He was going to keep His promise. He did intend to destroy the Evil One. She knew now that it may not be by this child, it may not be in her lifetime, but it was enough to know that her descendant would one day crush the serpent. In God's time He would fulfil the promise.

Chapter 4

" *L*eave your country, your people and your father's household and go to the land I will show you".

Along with the command God had given wonderful promises.

"I will make you into a great nation and I will bless you; I will make your name great, and you will be a blessing. I will bless those who bless you, and whoever curses you I will curse; and all peoples on earth will be blessed through you."

Where they were going they had no certain idea, nor did they know how long the journey would take. One thing only had been made clear to them; they were to go. It was a Divine Command.

They had left behind their beloved father. It had not been easy to say goodbye to the old man. They would have liked him to come too, but he was content to remain where he was. It was unlikely they would ever see him again, and their hearts were sorrowful on that account, but the Divine call had to be obeyed and they would not shirk from it.

"It will be an adventure," said Sarai bravely.

There was an element of excitement in setting out to go whither they knew not, albeit there was a little pulse of apprehension throbbing through Sarai's veins. What difficulties and dangers might lie ahead for them among a people whom they did not know, but who had the reputation of being wicked and idolatrous?

"Not that idolatry is anything new to us," thought Sarai.

It was all too familiar in the land of their nativity, but the family had kept themselves apart from all that, and there had been no inter-marriage with the Chaldeans. They had kept their spiritual worship intact by marrying within their own extended family, and the children of the marriages were in turn instructed and encouraged in the ways of the one true God, Yahwey.

"Children!"

Sarai sighed heavily as she reflected again on her own childless state. It had been her greatest sorrow that she had been unable to bear children, not only for her own sake, but for Abram's too. For years she had hoped against hope, but time was running out, and she knew it was becoming increasingly unlikely that she would conceive a child now at her age.

"Abram still hopes for a child, I know," Sarai said unhappily.

But he had been keen to bring Lot with them, and Sarai knew he looked on him almost as his own. Since Lot's father had died many years ago Abram had taken the boy under his wing, and it was understandable that he would want to bring him with him. If he had left him with his grandfather Terah in Haran who knew what might become of him?

Sarai sighed again. She hoped Abram would not be disappointed in his nephew, for he loved him dearly, but with a woman's intuition she sensed that Lot was far more interested in acquiring wealth than seeking after a deeper knowledge of God. Abram was so God-centred that it would not occur to him that Lot might not want to know God in the way that he did.

Sarai glanced over at the two men as they rode on the outskirts of the herd. Abram's erect dignified bearing, she reflected, was synonymous with his character. Strong and disciplined, yet kind and caring, he was a man who commanded respect. From the humblest of his servants to the noblest citizens of Ur and Haran, Abram had been held in high esteem.

"As for Lot, he will never be a man like his uncle," thought Sarai wryly.

In the azure sky the sun was shining almost directly overhead, and a faint blue haze shimmered just beyond them, creating an occasional mirage. It made Sarai think longingly of shady trees and a long cool drink of water. She glanced at Abram again and he answered her unspoken question with a nod.

"The sun grows hot," he said. "We will stop as soon as we reach the grove of trees on yonder hill."

They rode on in silence for a few minutes, then as they reached the trees Abram alighted from his camel and helped Sarai dismount. The servants were already spreading coverings on the ground under the shade, and gratefully Sarai seated herself and had a refreshing drink from her water skin.

"It is so good to rest out of the hot sun," she breathed thankfully.

In all their frequent stops in this long journey they always looked for a clump of trees where they could rest from the noon-tide heat and rise refreshed when the sun waned. This wooded hillside was an ideal spot, and far below, the sunlit valleys showed no signs of human habitation. Many beautiful terebinth trees, with their large dark leaves offered generous shade under their wide-spreading branches. Sarai lay back, her eyes closed, and allowed the stillness and tranquility of this delightful place to steal over her.

When she awoke it was late afternoon, and the servants were beginning to make preparations for the evening meal. Sarai arose and walked over to where Abram was instructing his men-servants to erect the tents and gather sticks for a fire.

"This is a good place to stay," Abram told her. "There are no Canaanite settlements near-by, and in any case we are hidden from sight in this little valley among the hills. The land offers good grazing for our livestock, and there is a brook which will supply us with water. The trees will give shelter and shade, and there is plenty of wood for fires."

Sarai smiled. Abram had thought of everything as always. She moved away to instruct her maids in the preparation of food, and they bustled about fetching water, kneading dough, attending to the fire, and soon the delicious aroma of cooking filled the air, while the smoke curled upwards from the burning wood and drifted skyward in the balmy breeze.

The meal over, Sarai sat at the door of her tent to enjoy the coolness of the evening, and watch the gold and crimson splendour of the setting sun as it sank in the vivid sky. She always felt a sense of privilege that she was able to share in the sun's last great moments of glory before it finally disappeared from sight behind the hills.

"This place is the most beautiful we have yet seen since coming into Canaan," Sarai observed.

"Yes," agreed Abram. "It will be a pleasant place to stay, and I believe it is called Shechem."

It was a ridge of high land between two greater mountains, and from its height they could see far and wide. Gently rolling hills with narrow valleys in between them stretched away into the distance, interspersed here and there with gleaming silvery streams which wound their way down the mountain slopes.

As evening melted into night the sky darkened to deep blue, then indigo, and serenity descended upon the land. Unobtrusively the first evening star appeared, and then gradually, as the sky darkened still further, a myriad of stars twinkled above in the blackness of the night-sky. Sarai caught her breath at the beauty of it all.

Presently Abram returned from his walk. He had been away a long time, but this was not unusual for he loved the beauty of evening as Sarai did, and often he would linger under the starry sky to meditate and pray before returning to the tent to sleep.

Tonight as he came in Sarai could sense his excitement and joy.

"God has spoken to me again!" he told her. "He was there Sarai. I could feel His presence."

"What did He say?" breathed Sarai.

"He said, 'To your offspring I will give this land'."

Abram's voice trembled with emotion. To have met with God and heard Him speak was an indescribable joy.

Sarai did not reply. She could feel the tears pricking her eyes and turned away. God had said He would give this land to Abram's offspring.

"But we have no offspring!" thought Sarai despairingly. "What does God mean?"

Why did He not give her children? Was this to be a life-long sorrow to her? And what about Abram? How did he feel? He wanted children as desperately as she did.

"Perhaps I could still. . ."

But it was a momentary thought.

Somehow she found it hard to believe that she would yet bear children after all these years of barrenness.

As she lay in the darkness and pondered these things she wished she could understand what God intended for them. She and Abram could trace their ancestry right back to Noah, and even beyond to Adam and Eve. Their branch of the family had always been worshippers of the Lord God. Stories of the creation, the serpent and the promise had been handed down for generations and they knew them all. It was their dearest wish to perpetuate their faith in God to succeeding generations.

"But how is that to be done if we do not have any children?" puzzled Sarai.

What did the future hold for them, and how was it possible for Abram to have offspring if she, Sarai was barren? If God did not give her children of her own there was only one way left to her, but Sarai resolutely refused to think of it.

What was it God had said to Abram?

"To your offspring I will give this land."

Perhaps she, Sarai would have no part to play in that.

Chapter 5

They had been journeying south for weeks. The green and pleasant hills around Bethel had provided lush pasture for their flocks, and Sarai would have been content to stay. Abram had built an altar to the Lord there, but he was consumed with a restless energy to continue and see more of the land to which God had told him to come.

"When we have seen all the land we can choose a place to settle down," he told Sarai. "I have heard from travellers that there is rich pasture-land down in the Negev region. We will go and see. When we find good pasture we can stop."

"How long will it take us?" wondered Sarai after Abram had gone out.

As they made their slow progress, hampered as they were by their large flocks of sheep and goats, they gradually became aware that the grass was less and less plentiful, and the looked-for rains had failed to come. The ground was becoming parched and barren, streams and brooks were drying up, and the burning sun shone down upon them day after day out of a cloudless sky.

As days merged into weeks, and weeks into months, the situation grew dire. The animals had become lean and weak, and the dry scorching heat seemed to sap what energy they had left, making it necessary to travel at an even slower pace. They covered little ground each day and still they journeyed southward.

To the left lay the desert, bleak, barren and inhospitable. On the right the land was bare, stripped of her bounty by the skeletal hand of drought. The fields and hills craved water but there was none. Behind them they had left the ground denuded and stark. Before them the earth had suffered the same grim fate.

"What are we going to do Abram?" worried Sarai.

Abram did not answer immediately.

"We are facing famine," he said finally. "There is nothing to do but go on Sarai, until we find water and pasture."

"Yes," Sarai acknowledged, sighing heavily.

It was true. There was nothing they could do but go on. There was little left of the stores they had brought with them; a few olives, figs and almonds; not enough to satisfy the gnawing pangs of hunger. They had such hopes of finding abundance in the Negev, but instead they found themselves experiencing severe famine.

"What is to become of us?" she moaned softly to herself.

How far would they have to travel before they found relief? Would they die of starvation in this desolate country? What about God's promises now? Had He not said He would bless them and give them this land?

Sarai's mind wrestled with these thoughts as she rode alongside Abram and Lot, but as if in answer to her unspoken question an unexpected solution suddenly presented itself. As they travelled on in the sultry heat they came upon a caravan of camels laden with goods.

Occasionally before they had met travellers coming from the south, and always they had stopped to greet them, listened to what news they had of foreign lands, and bought some of their produce.

Now Sarai's eyes lit up for the first time in weeks as they reached the travellers and saw the bulging loads strapped to the camels. She looked at Abram and found him smiling broadly.

"You will eat well this evening Sarai," he told her cheerfully. "Instruct the servants to light a fire."

It did not take Abram long to agree a price with the traders, and as silver and goods changed hands, the bundles were quickly unwrapped to reveal flour and oil, spices, fruit, dates and many other delicacies.

Joyfully Sarai and her maids set about preparing a feast, and before long the tantalising smell of fresh bread baking on the fire filled their nostrils. As soon as it was cooked they squatted on the dry ground and ate hungrily. Never had food tasted so good! There was the juice of fresh citrus fruit to drink which quenched their thirst in a most satisfying way, and revived their spirits.

As was customary they offered hospitality to the traders, who in turn entertained them with tales of Egypt and the wonderful sights they had seen there. Abram questioned them closely, and when he heard how there was food in abundance on the well-watered plains of the River Nile he drew Sarai and Lot aside.

"We will go to Egypt," he told them. "Just until the drought is over. When there is water in the streams again and pasture for our livestock we will return."

"How long will it take to reach Egypt?" enquired Sarai, smiling at the joyous prospect of abundance once again.

"We are close," Abram assured her. "The men say four more days travelling will be enough. We will have to travel slowly with the animals, but we will make an early start. Can you be ready at first light Sarai?"

Sarai smiled and nodded. For the first night in weeks she slept soundly and awakened before dawn eager to start the journey that would take them into Egypt.

They took the caravan trail which veered south-west and followed the well-beaten track that led towards the mysterious land of the Nile. It was not without a certain amount of trepidation and heightened anticipation that they approached the boundary between the two countries as they wondered what lay ahead of them in the land of the Pharaohs.

Sarai wondered if they would encounter the Pharaoh about whom they had heard so much. In all probability they would as Abram was a wealthy man, and would not escape notice as he travelled with his large herds and train of servants. It was not as though they could slip into the country un-noticed, graze their flocks for a period, and leave again when it suited them.

As they rode in silence under the blazing sun Sarai could see that Abram looked more and more ill at ease the closer they came to this foreign land. Several times he looked towards her as if to say something, but each time he turned away without speaking. Knowing him as she did Sarai perceived there was something on his mind, so finally she spoke.

"What is it Abram?" she enquired.

"Sarai, I know what a beautiful woman you are. When the Egyptians see you, they will say, 'This is his wife.' Then they will kill me but will let you live."

Sarai looked at him aghast.

"Abram, what are you saying?"

"Say you are my sister, so that I will be treated well for your sake and my life will be spared because of you."

Shocked, Sarai stared at him silently, trying to take in what he had just said.

"You are a very beautiful woman Sarai," he repeated, looking at her earnestly.

"But my youth has gone. I am no longer young Abram," she countered.

"Nevertheless, you are still beautiful," Abram said softly. "And your maturity gives you a poise and dignity that younger women do not possess."

Sarai smiled faintly, but quickly her eyes clouded over. Here was a situation she had not considered, but as always Abram thought of everything. If they did not practise this deception Abram could die. And if they did, what of her? She could become one of Pharaoh's con- cubines. Life could be very comfortable in an Egyptian palace, she had no doubt. It would offer a life of ease with all the little luxuries a woman loves, but there was an element of danger too. Pharaoh might want to take her as one of his wives and what would they do then? The thought was abhorrent to her for she loved Abram, but he was so anxious, and she could not find it in her heart to refuse.

"Have I really a choice?" she wondered silently.

If she did not consent to pose as his sister, and insisted on maintaining her married status would she occasion the death of her husband?

"I will do as you ask," she told him simply.

Abram smiled at her with gratitude and said no more.

As the journey continued both became silent, lost in their own thoughts. Sarai hoped against hope that the situation would not arise. Perhaps Abram was worrying needlessly.

Still, from what they had heard from passing travellers it seemed more likely than not. Kings regarded it as their privilege to take whatever woman they chose, and a king as imperial as the Egyptian Pharaoh would certainly insist on his rights.

The sun was almost at its mid-day strength, and the dust and heat were well-nigh unbearable. Weary and parched with thirst they needed to stop and rest. The sheep and goats were bleating pitifully, and the oxen and donkeys were panting for water. As yet there was no sign of the fertile plains they longed to see; only the sandy desert which seemed to stretch endlessly before them, so they knew they must press on if they were to reach a watering place before sundown.

This was their fourth day of travelling since they had met the caravan, and if the traders were right they should soon reach the river.

"We can stop only for a very short rest," Abram decided.

He helped Sarai down from her camel and she reached for her water skin. There was not much of the precious liquid left so she had to content herself with a sip or two. The servants brought some fruit, and she and Abram walked a little distance to stretch their limbs.

"Sarai," Abram began, "I would not ask you to pose as my sister if it were not necessary."

Sarai assumed a confidence she did not feel.

"It may not be necessary," she rejoined, trying to smile.

"I fear it will be," Abram replied. "But I will come for you as soon as possible. Once the famine is over and Canaan can support us again we will return."

"But what if . . . if Pharaoh does not wish . . . to release me?" she asked hesitantly.

"I will find a way." said Abram firmly.

Without saying another word he strode away. After issuing some brief commands to the servants he returned.

"We must go," he told her briefly.

The sun burned fiercely upon them as they slowly made their way onward. Sarai grew dizzy with the heat and glare of the sun. She felt as if they were on a never-ending journey which would go on until they died. She had lost all hope that they would ever see green fields or blue rivers again. She tried to visualise lush grass, fruit-bearing trees, colourful flowers, but she seemed to be floating in a sea of sand from which she would never be able to rise. She could not rouse herself from the drifting sensation.

"Sarai, Sarai, wake up!"

Sarai opened her eyes with an effort. Abram was riding alongside her looking excited.

"We are nearing journey's end Sarai," he told her. "Soon you will be able to rest. Look around you."

Sarai's eyes opened wide as she saw that instead of the sandy rocky landscape that had surrounded them for days, there now appeared occasional palm trees, odd splashes of colour here and there, and little tufts of grass everywhere. These hopeful signs revived her greatly and she urged her camel forward eagerly.

Gradually the land changed completely. Trees and grass were becoming more and more plentiful, and

Sarai was sure they must soon come within sight of the river.

She was not disappointed. A splash of blue in the distance caught her eye.

"The river!" she shouted, forgetting her weariness in her joy and excitement.

Sarai jumped down from her camel without waiting for Abram's help. Leaving him to follow more sedately with Lot, she kicked off her sandals as she ran, and threw off her head covering which had protected her from the sun. Joyously she splashed the cool water around her face and bare arms, as she stooped to cup it in her hands. How cool and refreshing it was on her skin! For days she had dreamed of this moment. How wonderful it was to be here at last after the weeks of drought and the tortuous journey!

Sarai turned to share the moment of happiness with Abram, her face alight with pleasure, her eyes shining with excitement.

Suddenly the smile froze on her face. Before her stood a tall bronze-skinned man with the unmistakable look of an Egyptian courtier. He looked at her appraisingly and Sarai felt a hot blush rising to her cheeks. It was clear from his expression he liked what he saw, and Sarai felt her heart begin to pound painfully. She glanced at Abram uncertainly, but he avoided her eyes. He turned to the Egyptian who looked at him questioningly.

"This is my sister," he said.

Chapter 6

A cool breeze wafted into the room. The fine white linen drapes fluttered gently as the soft wind caught them, and the heavy sensuous perfume of exotic flowers drifted in from the outer gardens. Egyptian slave girls fanned rhythmically to the sound of distant music. Sarai was not sure where it came from, but it was soothingly dream-like, and it gave her an eerie, other-worldly feeling as if it were not really she who was reclining in this luxurious room in the palace of the Pharaoh, but someone else. It was as if she was an onlooker, instead of a participant in this drama.

She had been here many days now, and she had not yet seen the Pharaoh for which she was profoundly thankful. The Egyptian girls in the king's harem had been friendly. She was older than most of them of course, but they treated her with respect. They acknowledged her undoubted beauty and did not seem jealous. They were all dark-eyed and black haired, while she was so very different looking.

"The princes say you are as regal as a queen," they told her. "They say when you walk your every movement is grace, and your face is as fair as any woman's they have ever seen."

Sarai smiled remotely. Often Abram had said those very things to her.

"How I wish I could be with him!" thought Sarai to herself.

He had been to the palace several times to visit her, but she could see him only as a brother. When they walked in the palace gardens they spoke of the livestock and of the fertile river valley where the sheep and oxen were becoming fat and sleek again. There was an abundance of food and water and life was very comfortable.

"But I miss you Sarai."

"And I you," whispered Sarai. "Oh, Abram, did we do the right thing?"

"Pharaoh has treated me exceedingly well, and it is because of you Sarai. I have acquired many more sheep and cattle, donkeys, camels and servants. As soon as the famine in Canaan is over we will return richer than we were."

Sarai's eyes filled with tears as Abram left. Much as she enjoyed the ease and luxury of life in Egypt she longed to return to Canaan. The feeling of unease would not leave her, and she was fearful lest their deception should be uncovered.

She knew it was only a matter of time until Pharaoh would send for her, and although it would be a great honour she did not wish to spend a night with the king of Egypt. She was married to Abram, it was he whom she loved, and had not God said that a man and wife were to be as one. They had not consulted Him when they decided to take this action. Abram had not suggested such a thing, and she had gone along with the deception, in spite of her misgivings, to ease Abram's mind. Now her conscience troubled her.

"I must think what to do if …if…the Pharaoh sends for me."

She reviewed her position. She had posed as an unmarried woman and had agreed to enter Pharaoh's palace. He had shown great kindness to her and to

Abram, and he would expect her to be compliant when he requested her company. The more she thought about it the more she realised that to give herself to him was unthinkable. But what was to be done? To refuse was impossible. To assent was to betray her husband, herself and her God.

"I cannot do it, I cannot do it." she groaned.

As she pondered the vexing question Sarai gradually came to see that there was only one thing to be done. She would place herself in God's hands. Had he not given hope to Adam and Eve in their darkest hour? The stories that had been handed down from generation to generation told of the faithfulness of God to those who put their trust in Him. He was a mighty God, a God to be feared, a God to be trusted. She too would put her trust in Him. With a lighter heart she retired to rest.

"I will trust my God," she whispered as she laid her head down to sleep.

As the days passed Sarai became aware of a change in manner among the other women in the harem. Where previously they had been open and friendly, now they appeared guarded and sullen. They no longer laughed and joked with her. She often caught strange looks between them when she appeared, and suddenly for no apparent reason they seemed to regard her with suspicion. Furthermore some of them were sick with a mysterious illness, and it was even rumoured that Pharaoh himself was ill.

"What is the matter with these women?" she asked once, but no one gave her an answer.

With the passing of time Sarai found herself left more and more alone. The other women made excuses to leave when she entered, and Sarai, confused, gave up the effort to engage them in conversation. What was going on in their superstitious minds, she wondered. Did they think she was an ill omen? Well, perhaps she was. She should not be here. She was certain now that she and Abram had been wrong to deceive the king. They should have trusted God to protect Abram in this land to which they had been forced to come because of the famine.

"God made wonderful promises to Abram," Sarai reminded herself. "Would He really have allowed any harm to come to him?"

Sarai paced up and down restlessly. If only she could get away from here, but she was trapped, forced to live a life of deception. She had, for a time, enjoyed the opulent luxury of Egypt, but she would gladly exchange it all for a tent on a wooded hillside in Canaan if the famine was over and she could be there with Abram.

Each day brought fresh news of another being stricken with illness in Pharaoh's household. Soon there would be no-one left who was not afflicted with this strange malady. It was clear that the women regarded her as being the cause of the disease, and they shunned her as if she had a plague. Only the Egyptian girl who had been given to her as a personal maid spoke to her now, and that only because she had no choice. She came daily to dress Sarai's hair and fan her during the hot afternoons.

"Hagar, what ails these people?" Sarai asked her one morning.

"They say your God has put a curse on Pharaoh's household," Hagar told her hesitantly. "He must be a very powerful god to curse Pharaoh."

For a moment Sarai sat in stunned silence. Then she smiled.

"He is!" she said.

Dismissing her maid, Sarai gave way to the emotions which engulfed her. So God was protecting her!. It was because of her that He had sent this sickness to the palace. Tears filled her eyes and overflowed. Feelings of gratitude and humility overcame her. God cared about her! Guilty as she was she felt undeserving of His goodness.

For a while she sat in reverent thankfulness, but soon a twinge of fear crept into her heart. What would happen now ? If it was common belief among his household that she was the cause of the curse, what did Pharaoh himself believe? Would he send for her to question her, or would he simply order her out of his house?

She did not have to wait long for the answer. Hagar had returned and stood before her nervously.

"The king's officials are waiting to escort you to the king," she told Sarai.

Instantly the curtains were drawn back and two of Pharaoh's courtiers entered unceremoniously. Sarai's mouth felt dry and her knees suddenly weakened.

"The king commands your immediate presence," they snapped. "Your husband is already with him."

Sarai gasped. So the Pharaoh already knew every-thing! They were at the mercy of the king of Egypt! Or were they? Only One was more powerful; the God of Abram and Sarai. The thought gave her courage, and with her head held high, she allowed the Egyptians to escort her into the presence of the king. Her heart was pounding painfully as she bowed deeply before him.

Pharaoh looked at her, his face softening for a moment as he beheld her beautiful countenance, then he turned angrily to Abram who stood before him.

"What is this you have done to me?" he stormed furiously. "Why did you not tell me she was your wife? Why did you say, 'She is my sister'? I might have taken her to be my wife."

He paced up and down agitatedly for a few moments before turning fiercely to Abram again.

"Here is your wife," he shouted. "Take her and go your way!"

Sarai dared not look at Abram, but she knew how he would be feeling: guilty, ashamed, humiliated, before the king, before all these people, before God, before her. He had lied, he had failed to trust his God. Sarai knew that would lie heaviest on his heart.

"Take them away," yelled Pharaoh. "Make sure they leave the country. Today!"

Ignominiously Sarai found herself being ushered out of the king's presence along with Abram. Only one thought sustained her. God had vindicated her trust!.

Chapter 7

This time there was no doubt where they were going. With the humiliation of Egypt behind them there was only one place where they could find renewal.

"Bethel," Abram said simply. "We will go to Bethel, the house of the Lord."

"Yes," agreed Sarai.

The distance was long and the journey tiresome, but travel-weary as she was Sarai knew Abram would not rest until he worshipped at God's altar, and sought His forgiveness and blessing as he called on His Name once again in that holy place. Sarai herself had cause for deep thankfulness.

Progress was painfully slow as Abram had greatly increased his flocks, herds and servants in Egypt thanks to the generosity of the Pharaoh.

"Before he ordered us out of his country!" thought Sarai wryly.

In addition Lot accompanied them with all his possessions, but at last they reached Bethel and pitched their tents. With their souls restored and their bodies refreshed, Sarai hoped they would be able to stay in this pleasant place, but it was not long before it became clear that this might not be possible. Returning one day from the fields Abram confirmed Sarai's fears.

"There is simply not enough room for us all here Sarai. Lot's herdsmen are quarrelling with my herdsmen, so I have given Lot his choice of the land, and he has chosen the whole plain around the River Jordan."

"The best well-watered land, just like the land of Egypt!" thought Sarai. "He would!"

Aloud she said, "You are too generous Abram."

"I do not begrudge it to him Sarai, but it saddens me that he has chosen to live near Sodom. It is well-known for its wickedness, and I fear he may ...."

Abram's voice trailed off and his face wore a solemn look.

"And what about us Abram?" queried Sarai. "Where are we to go?"

"Come with me to the top of the hill Sarai. You will see."

The view was breathtaking. The whole land stretched out in every direction with rocky peaks, rolling hills and tree-covered valleys.She could see the broad plain of the Jordan River to the east where Lot had chosen to settle, but to the south and west there was sufficient pasture for their livestock with little or no human habitation, and she could see what Abram meant. Even though Lot had the benefit of the river, there would be springs among the rocks, streams in the hills and lush pasture-land in the valleys.

Abram was speaking again and Sarai turned from surveying the countryside to listen to what he was saying.

"After Lot left God spoke to me again," he said slowly.

"What did he say?" asked Sarai with some trepidation.

"God said, 'Look north and south, east and west. All the land that you see I will give to you and your off-spring forever. I will make your offspring like the dust of the earth, so that if anyone could count the dust, then your offspring could be counted'."

Sarai caught her breath sharply and turned away quickly. Such words always cut deeply into her soul since she had no children. What did God mean when He spoke of offspring when they did not have any?

Abram appeared not to notice Sarai's discomfort. With excitement in his voice he was speaking again.

"God said, 'Go, walk through the length and breadth of the land, for I am giving it to you'."

Clearly Abram was thrilled. Sarai tried to smile for his sake even though she did not feel like it, and she knew this meant they would be on the move again.

"When do we set out Abram?" she asked quietly.

"In a few days," Abram said as they went down the hill together.

He went to instruct the servants, and Sarai sat in her tent, puzzling over this latest vision of Abram's and trying to make sense of the words God had spoken.

"I will make your offspring like the dust of the earth," God had said.

It seemed unimaginable to Sarai. How could this be? They had been in this land for ten years and in that time they still had no offspring, nor did they own any of the land. God had promised both. Sarai sat silently, her mind wrestling with these words of God until Abram came in.

"Sarai, do not look so sad," he said gently. "The whole land is before us. We will find a pleasant place to live."

Sarai lay awake long into the night, turning over in her mind the questions that seemingly had no answers. Abram had assured her they would find a place to settle, but he had not referred to their childlessness, though she knew it troubled him too.

In the morning they began preparing for their departure, and the following day they set off once more, travelling south until they came at last to a sheltered valley surrounded by gentle hills, with the most magnificent trees they had ever seen, and a splendid view of the distant mountains to the north and west.

Sarai knew she would love those trees, and it cheered her spirit considerably. They would provide shade from the heat of the sun,and shelter when the wind and rain came. They discovered the place was called Mamre and it was near the small town of Hebron.

Abram's first task was to build an altar to the Lord, and there they worshipped, Sarai with a thankful heart that they could finally settle down, at least for a time.

They were not long encamped at Mamre when a sudden emergency occurred. A battle instigated by some petty kings in the land resulted in the capture of Lot and all that he had. Where his nephew was concerned Abram was always instantly protective so he immediately set out with his retinue of over three hundred trained servants and rescued Lot, the nearest he had to a son.

What happened next was an awesome encounter between Abram and God, after which Sarai made the decision she had hoped she would never have to make.

God had spoken gracious words to Abram in a vision.

"Do not be afraid Abram. I am your shield, your very great reward."

Abram had broached the subject of his childlessness with God.

"O Sovereign Lord, what can You give me since I remain childless, and the one who will inherit my estate is Eliezer of Damascus. You have given me no children, so a servant in my household will be my heir."

God graciously replied, "This man will not be your heir, but a son coming from your own body will be your heir."

In his vision God then took Abram outside into the dark starry night.

"Look up at the heavens and count the stars–if indeed you can count them. So shall your offspring be."

It had amazed and thrilled Abram, but when he told Sarai about it she listened in disbelief, and pain throbbed in her heart, leaving her sad and confused.

God at that time also gave Abram further assurance that he would inherit the land.

"I am the Lord who brought you out of Ur of the Chaldeans," He told him, "to give you this land to take possession of it."

God then did something amazing. He made a covenant with Abram in a solemn ceremony after sunset when darkness had fallen, asking no commitment from Abram, but taking upon Himself the fulfilment of the covenant. God uttered prophetic words regarding Abram's descendants, and then He gave His promise.

"To your descendants I give this land, from the river of Egypt to the great river, the Euphrates."

Sarai believed devoutly in God, but she could not understand why He had left her childless in view of all these promises. Why, why, why?. Everything He had said to Abram about having a son of his own had not come to pass. She put her head in her hands and wept tears of sorrow and longing.

"I find it so hard to believe," she whispered to herself. "I am too old. I know I am."

She sat long under the trees, distressed in soul and weary with crying. With every fibre of her being she longed for a child. Why, in spite of all His promises had He left her childless? Surely He, who knew everything, knew how desperately she longed for a baby.

In her distress Sarai arose and walked back and forth under the trees. For a long time she paced the ground in agony of soul until the shadows lengthened and the sun began to lower in the west. She had wrestled until she had come to a decision. God had said he would give Abram a son coming from his own body. Very well! There was only one thing to be done, and it was up to her to do it.

She made her way back to their settlement, and met Abram coming from the fields. Quickly before she might change her mind she spoke.

"Abram," she said bluntly. "The Lord has kept me from having children. I will give you my maid Hagar as your wife. Perhaps I can build a family through her."

Abram looked at her steadily for a long moment. Finally he nodded, and Sarai, choking back her tears walked quickly away.

Chapter 8

*I*t was not long before Sarai realised she had made a terrible mistake. As soon as Hagar became pregnant with Abram's child she began to show her contempt for her mistress.

Abram! He had been quick to agree to the arrangement!

"Why could he not have seen what it would do to me?" she fumed as she paced back and forth . It was all his fault.

As soon as he appeared back from the fields Sarai vented the full force of her fury upon him.

"You are responsible for the wrong I am suffering," she raged. "I put my servant in your arms and now that she knows she is pregnant, she despises me. May the Lord judge between you and me."

"Your servant is in your hands," Abram replied quietly and calmly. "Do with her whatever you think best."

Sarai was taken aback. He was accepting her accusation without a word in his own defence. She did not know what to say. Staring at him for a moment, she then turned on her heel and walked quickly away.

He was right! Hagar was her servant and she could do with her as she liked. She did not have to put up with her contempt!

"How dare she mock me!" she raged as she rushed to find her. "She is my servant and she has no right to treat me like this. I will show her who is mistress."

In the days that followed Sarai mercilessly pursued her assault on her maid until finally Hagar could take it no longer and ran away. Sarai was neither surprised nor sorry.

With the cause of her pain at least out of her sight Sarai had ample opportunity to calm down and think things over. She began to understand that her unreasonable behaviour had been the result of her highly emotional state.

Hagar's pregnancy had been the intended outcome of her union with Abram, which Sarai herself had instigated, but when it had come to pass, the reality of it hurt much more than she could ever have imagined. That Hagar was pregnant by Abram when it should have been she who was carrying Abram's child was more than she could bear. All the pent-up longings of her own unfulfilled hopes and dreams suddenly spilled over, and she had lashed out at her husband in her pain.

Her anger spent, she felt ashamed of her conduct, especially towards Abram.

"Your servant is in your hands," had been Abram's response which had surprised and pleased her.

Considerately, Abram did not point out that she had given this woman to him in the hope of obtaining a child through her. Instead he acknowledged her as Sarai's servant to do with as she saw fit. He had shown understanding and care for Sarai, and her heart had softened.

"It is why I love him," she smiled to herself.

What she had done had been out of love for him of course, so that he could have a son, and he was not entirely guiltless since he had willingly agreed to the plan. She wondered how he felt now that the mother of his unborn child had gone, but they had not spoken of it since Hagar's departure.

Sarai did not expect ever to see Hagar again, and she felt guilty on that count since Abram would never see his child, but she had reckoned without God, for one day, totally out of the blue, Hagar returned, submissive and much changed apparently by her encounter with God in the desert where He had heard her cry for help.

Ashamed of her earlier cruelty Sarai left Hagar to herself until the child was born. He was named Ishmael in obedience to God's instruction and in acknowledgement that "God hears" when the cries of the helpless come before Him.

"Yes," mused Sarai. "God hears." She remembered her plea to God in her plight in Pharaoh's palace in Egypt.

Abram was delighted with his son, but for Sarai the birth of this child brought all her longings for motherhood to the surface once again, and she took no further interest in the boy. He was Hagar's to care for and Abram's to enjoy. She had no part in him.

Abram had his son. She had done what she had to do to make God's promise come true, but at great cost to herself. She was still a barren wife, while her servant was the mother of her husband's child, and he could rejoice in being a father.

"Does Abram still love me as much as he used to?" she wondered wistfully.

The child had made a difference in his life. He would watch this boy grow to manhood and would bestow upon him all the love he had hitherto given to his nephew Lot. This boy, as Abram's son, would inherit the Covenant blessings that God had promised Abram and his descendants forever, and Sarai would have no part in that. It made her feel left out, excluded.

"I feel as if ....as if....my life is not worth much," she concluded sadly.

Chapter 9

$\mathcal{S}$arai sat under her beloved terebinth trees in a daze, not knowing whether to laugh or cry. It had been the most astonishing day! God had spoken to Abram many times before, but this time was completely different. This time God spoke of her by name, and made the most astounding prediction that Sarai could scarcely take it in.

First of all God spoke directly to Abram.

"I am God Almighty; walk before Me and be blameless. I will confirm My covenant between Me and you, and will greatly increase your numbers."

Abram had fallen on his face before God in reverence while God continued to speak.

"As for Me, this is My covenant with you: You will be the father of many nations. No longer will you be called Abram; your name will be Abraham, for I have made you a father of many nations. I will make you very fruitful; I will make nations of you, and kings will come from you. I will establish My covenant as an everlasting covenant between Me and you and your descendants after you for the generations to come, to be your God and the God of your descendants after you."

That in itself was amazing, but it was the words God spoke concerning herself that Sarai found so incredible.

"As for Sarai your wife, you are no longer to call her Sarai; her name will be Sarah. I will bless her and will surely give you a son by her. I will bless her so that she will be the mother of nations; kings of peoples will come from her."

"I will...surely give you a son by her," Sarah repeated to herself. Oh, if only! But it seemed impossible!

Even Abraham had expressed his incredulity over this statement.

"Will a son be born to a man a hundred years old? Will Sarah bear a child at the age of ninety?" He had said the words to himself and laughed at the thought of it.

Aloud he said to God, "If only Ishmael might live under Your blessing!"

"Yes," God had said, "but your wife Sarah will bear you a son, and you will call him Isaac. I will establish My covenant with him as an everlasting covenant for his descendants after him."

God had even chosen a name for the son Sarah and Abraham would have together.

"If only it could be true!" breathed Sarah. "But I will be ninety next year! No-one has a child at ninety!"

But why would God say this if He did not mean it? Sarah struggled to understand the words God had spoken. She loved the things He had said. He had renamed her Sarah. It meant 'princess', and that gave her a dignity she had not felt for a very long time. He said she would be a mother of nations, and that kings would come from her.

Best of all God had said He would establish His covenant with her son Isaac. It would be an everlasting covenant for all the descendants of Isaac, God had promised, when as yet there was no Isaac.

Sarah lay back on the grass with her arms behind her head and allowed herself to daydream.

"A son, a son of my own," Sarah mused with a half-smile on her lips. "It would be so wonderful!"

She herself would be a princess with kings as her descendants. Her son would inherit the blessing, and not Ishmael. Sarah smiled broadly at the thought. But God had plans for Ishmael too. What was it He had said about him?

"As for Ishmael, I have heard you," He had said to Abraham. "I will surely bless him; I will make him fruitful and will greatly increase his numbers. He will be the father of twelve rulers, and I will make him into a great nation."

At least Abraham would be happy at the prospects for his son Ishmael, but Sarah laughed aloud when she recalled the next words God had spoken.

"But My covenant I will establish with Isaac, whom Sarah will bear to you by this time next year."

"Next year! I could be a mother in a year's time!"

For a few blissful minutes she contemplated the thought. To hold her own baby in her arms! More than anything in the world she wished it would come to pass, but how could it be? It seemed impossible.

It was twelve years since Ishmael had been born. All those years ago Sarah had been so upset over Hagar's ability to give Abraham a son when she could not, but through the years she had reached acceptance of the situation. But now, now she had been given a glimmer of hope. It was almost too much to bear.

The golden glow of the lowering sun sent shafts of light through the dark green foliage of the trees. It was time to go.

Sarah rose reluctantly. She would have to leave her beautiful daydreams behind, and face reality again. She was not the mother of a son. Abraham's son was not hers. That was Hagar's privilege. She was the barren wife, and in less than a year she would be ninety years old. To give birth to a child at that age seemed utterly impossible. And yet.....

God had said, "Sarah will have a son."

Dare she believe it?

"At least I have a new name," said Sarah with satisfaction. "I am a princess!"

Chapter 10

The mid-day sun was at its height, and Sarah and Abraham had taken refuge from its heat in the shade of their tent. They sat at the entrance where they could enjoy any little breeze that rustled through the tall trees nearby. They sat in silence, each thinking their own thoughts.

Suddenly they became aware of three men standing before them. Abraham immediately jumped up and rushed to greet them, while Sarah retreated a little further into the tent so that she could observe them. There was something unusual about them, and watching them, Sarah realised they were no ordinary men. As soon as Abraham spoke this was confirmed.

"If I have found favour in your eyes, my lord, do not pass your servant by. Let a little water be brought, and then you may all wash your feet and rest under this tree. Let me get you something to eat, so you can be refreshed and then go on your way—now that you have come to your servant."

"Very well," they answered. "Do as you say."

Abraham hurried into the tent to Sarah.

"Quick," he said. "Get three seahs of fine flour and knead it and bake some bread."

Sarah knew by the urgency in his tone that these were extremely important visitors, so she hastened to knead the bread and prepare it for the guests.

Meanwhile Abraham ran to the herd to select a choice tender calf which he gave to a servant to prepare.

When all was ready Abraham himself served the men with the roasted meat, fresh bread, curds and milk, and courteously stood under a tree while he watched them eat. Sarah too, watched from the entrance of the tent, and straightened up quickly when she suddenly heard her name mentioned.

"Where is Sarah your wife?" asked the men.

"There, in the tent," replied Abraham.

As she listened Sarah heard amazing words, spoken very graciously and simply.

"I will surely return to you about this time next year, and Sarah your wife will have a son."

Sarah's immediate response was to laugh to herself as she thought, "After I am worn out and my husband is old, will I now have this pleasure?"

She had not even spoken her thoughts aloud, but the next words Sarah heard filled her with fear and awe, for she quickly realised that this was none other than the Lord Himself speaking.

"Why did Sarah laugh and say, 'Will I really have a child, now that I am old?' Is anything too hard for the Lord? I will return to you at the appointed time and Sarah will have a son."

Sarah could see immediately that her laughter, inward though it was, had shown disrespect to the Lord and she hastily tried to deny it.

"I did not laugh," she lied.

But it was useless to lie to God. He was the Almighty God of creation, and He knew the innermost thoughts of Sarah's heart.

"Yes you did laugh," He said.

Ashamed, Sarah said nothing more, and as she meditated on the conversation her heart stirred within her, and she felt deeply moved that the Lord had deigned to speak to her. How could she be so arrogant as to try to lie to God, especially when He had imparted such an amazing promise?

"Is anything too hard for the Lord?" He had said.

Sarah turned these words over and over in her mind as she contemplated the power of God in relation to the promise He had made.

This was the same promise He had given to Abraham a short time ago, and she had not dared to believe it. Now she had heard it for herself, the beautiful, gracious words spoken by God Himself, and she had been foolish enough to laugh, and worse, to lie to God about it. Yet He, in His kindness, repeated the promise. How could she dare to disbelieve it?

At first Sarah wept over her unbelief and arrogance towards God. Then as she continued to meditate on the wonderful words He had spoken, her eyes grew dreamy, and a tender smile played about her lips.

"Sarah will have a son!" The most beautiful words in the world!

"I will be a mother in a year's time!" said Sarah in awe.

Later when she and Abraham talked it over they both acknowledged that the power of God could bring this about even though it seemed impossible.

"I believe Him Sarah," said Abraham decisively. "The son we will have together will be the son of God's promise."

"I believe Him too," Sarah responded softly. "Oh Abraham, it is so wonderful!"

As she lay down to sleep that night her mind was still occupied with the wonder of God's promise. A son! That had been her dearest wish all through her married life. She had taken matters into her own hands years ago in an effort to make God's promise come true, and she had been the one to suffer. Why had she not trusted God?

"I trust Him now," she smiled to herself. "Now, through the power and goodness of God, it will come to pass."

After such an amazing day Sarah was dismayed the following morning when Abraham announced they would be moving in order to find fresh pasture for the animals. Sarah was sorry to leave Mamre with its beautiful sheltering trees, but such were the necessities of the pastoral life when grass was scarce.

They travelled into the Negev region again, and eventually pitched their tents in a place called Gerar, having obtained permission from the king.

"Sarah," said Abraham quietly, "I have told the king of Gerar that you are my sister."

Sarah gasped, but she knew there was no use in protesting so she said nothing. She had agreed when they were in Egypt, so Abraham had obviously taken her assent this time for granted.

Abraham did not say anything more, and went out to speak to his servant, but when he had gone Sarah burst into tears and sobbed into her cushions for a long time.

"How could he do this again, especially now when... when God has given us such a promise? Why is he so afraid?"

It was puzzling. Had not God spoken to him many times and given him wonderful assurances of His blessing with the promise of descendants and land? Would the king of Gerar really kill him so that he could take his wife? Surely God would protect him! Had not Abraham said he believed God's promises? It was inexplicable that Abraham felt he needed to do this.

They were scarcely settled when Abimelech sent for Sarah. It was with much trepidation and reluctance that she consented to go, but courageously she decided at the beginning that she would put her trust in God, and in due time her trust was rewarded.

When she was called into the king's presence Abimelech, along with his officials, was already challenging Abraham.

"What have you done to us?" he said. "How have I wronged you that you have brought such guilt upon me and my kingdom? You have done things to me that should not be done."

Abimelech paced up and down before stopping again in front of Abraham.

"What was your reason for doing this?" he demanded.

Abraham, embarrassed, explained, "I said to myself, 'There is surely no fear of God in this place, and they will kill me because of my wife.' Besides, she really is my sister, the daughter of my father though not of my mother; and she became my wife. And when God caused me to wander from my father's household, I said to her, 'This is how you can show your love to me: Everywhere we go, say of me, "He is my brother."'"

Abimelech stared silently at Abraham, and Sarah held her breath. Then he said generously, "My land is before you. Live wherever you like."

Turning to Sarah, Abimelech said, "I am giving your brother a thousand shekels of silver. This is to cover the offence against you before all who are with you; You are completely vindicated."

"Abimelech has shown himself to be an honourable man, more honourable than my husband," Sarah thought, albeit a little guiltily, for she did not want to be disloyal to Abraham, but God had told him to walk before Him and be blameless, yet he had deceived the king. Abimelech's rebuke had been merited.

As they left the king's presence Sarah let out a deep breath of thankfulness. Once again God had protected her.

Chapter 11

*S*arah lay back on her cushions and laughed, a joyous, happy laugh, the laugh of a woman who has been given one of life's best gifts; a child of her own. She looked down tenderly at the tiny figure lying beside her and laughed again for sheer joy.

"God has brought me laughter," she said, "and everyone who hears about this will laugh with me."

She had waited a long time for this precious baby. She had come to this country childless, and now at last, twenty-five years later, at the age of ninety the miracle had happened. Sarah acknowledged that it was God and He alone whose power had enabled her to conceive and give birth to this child. It truly was a miracle.

"Little Isaac," she said, gently kissing his soft cheek. "God gave you your name, and you are well named! You have brought me such joy."

Abraham too was beside himself with happiness. This baby was the promised child of the Covenant. God had fulfilled His word.

Still chuckling to herself Sarah said, "Who would have said to Abraham that Sarah would nurse children? Yet I have borne him a son in his old age."

Day by day the baby grew and thrived. When he was eight days old Abraham came for him to perform on him the rite of circumcision as the sign of the Covenant in accordance with God's instruction. Sarah wept at the thought of her precious baby being subjected to it, but it took only a few minutes, and before long her baby was back in her arms again, sleeping soundly.

As the golden days of happiness went by Sarah enjoyed her baby to the full. The first time he smiled was a delight, then he was cooing and chuckling and making little sounds as he looked up at her.

"Oh, you are the sweetest little baby that ever was!" Sarah would croon over him.

Being a mother was wonderful! There was no greater fulfilment than having a child of your own. Abraham too adored him, and Sarah loved to watch them together. Isaac was the son from his own body God had promised him, borne by his wife and no other. This son was theirs together, and they, all three of them, were the people of the Covenant.

Sarah almost regretted his growing older. He was so delightful as a baby when she could pick him up and cuddle him, but he was cute as a toddler too, plodding around on his little feet, and finding interest in every-thing around him.

When it was time to wean him Sarah felt another pang of regret. Her baby was a baby no longer. He was growing up.

They held a great feast to celebrate his weaning. There was abundant food for everyone including Abraham's large retinue of servants, and it was a joyful occasion. Sarah, who scarcely took her eyes off her son as he played with some of the servants' children, suddenly noticed Hagar's son Ishmael edging closer to Isaac. She watched horrified as Ishmael began to tease and mock the small boy. Outraged, she rushed to rescue him, and then hurried determinedly to speak to Abraham.

"Get rid of that slave woman and her son," she said furiously, "for that slave woman's son will never share in the inheritance with my son Isaac."

She could see that Abraham was distressed, but at that moment she was too incensed to care.

"I suffered enough through that woman," she said bitterly. "Now her son is mocking my son, just as she mocked me, and I am not going to allow it."

The following morning when she awoke Abraham came into the tent.

"I have sent Hagar away with the boy," he informed Sarah heavily.

Sarah's heart went out to him for Ishmael was his son too, and it must have been hard for him to say good-bye.

"God spoke to me last night," Abraham went on. "He said, 'Do not be so distressed about the boy and your maidservant. Listen to whatever Sarah tells you, because it is through Isaac that your offspring will be reckoned.'"

Sarah smiled triumphantly. She was right! Isaac, and he alone was the child of the Covenant, and it would be his descendants who would inherit the blessings of the Covenant.

Her eyes glistened with tears of joy and thankfulness. She felt completely fulfilled. Her son, the son God had given to her, was the son of God's promise. With the slave woman and her son gone, Abraham, Isaac and she could settle down as the family they were meant to be, and enjoy God's blessing both now and in the future.

Chapter 12

*L*ate afternoon sunshine pervaded the valley, covering it with a golden glow. The fields were still and quiet. Sheep and goats were grazing peacefully while the young kids and lambs were chasing each other playfully. Birds sang, wild flowers flourished in abundance, and the little spring trickled gently down through the stones into a natural pool created by a deep chasm among the rocks. It was an idyllic pastoral scene, and the young woman who came each evening to draw water from the well delighted in the beauty and tranquility of it every time she came.

This evening as she approached the well she was surprised to find strangers with their camels waiting there. She counted ten camels, and they had been made to kneel in front of the well as if waiting to be watered. As she drew nearer she could see that one man, who was standing beside the spring, looked as if he was ..... could it be that he was praying?

When she reached the spring she swung her jar easily down from her shoulder and filled it with the clear pure water. The man who had been praying ended his petition and came hurrying to meet her.

"Please give me a little water from your jar," he said.

"Drink, my lord," she said, immediately lowering her jar to her hands and giving him a drink.

She watched him with satisfaction as he drank thirstily, and then she looked at the kneeling camels.

"I will draw water for your camels too, until they have finished drinking," she told him with a smile.

She poured the remaining water from her jar into the animals' drinking trough, and ran to fill it again and again until the camels finished drinking.

She was aware that the man was watching her closely as she sped back and forth from the well to the trough, but he looked kind and she found she did not mind his scrutiny. No doubt he was surprised and probably grateful that a young woman would take the trouble to draw water for his entire entourage, but they were parched and travel-weary she had no doubt, and she was happy to offer them this kindness.

"Where have they come from?" she wondered.

She filled her jar once more to take back to her family, and as she turned to speak to the stranger again, her eyes widened in surprise as he presented her with beautiful gold bracelets and a gold ring.

"Whose daughter are you?" he asked. "Please tell me, is there room in your father's house for us to spend the night?"

"I am the daughter of Bethuel, the son that Milcah bore to Nahor ," she replied, looking at him wonderingly.

"This man must have business with my father," she thought, looking down at the costly gifts he had bestowed upon her.

Remembering his request she told him, "We have plenty of straw and fodder, as well as room for you to spend the night."

At this the man bowed down and worshipped the Lord saying, "Praise be to the Lord, the God of my master Abraham, who has not abandoned His kindness and faithfulness to my master. As for me, the Lord has led me on the journey to the house of my master's relatives."

Abraham! Yes, she knew of him! So this was his chief servant, and he had sent him in quest of his relatives.

Rebekah ran quickly to her mother to tell her this exciting news, leaving the man to follow at a slower pace with his camels and servants. Rebekah's brother Laban, seeing the gold jewellery on his sister's arms, realised that this was an important visitor, and he took it upon himself to welcome him.

"Come, you who are blessed by the Lord," he said genially. "Why are you standing out here? I have prepared the house and a place for the camels."

He immediately gave orders to his servants to attend to the camels and bring water to wash the feet of the head servant and his men. Then he brought them in and set food before them, but their guest refused.

"I will not eat until I have told you what I have to say."

He looked around them all while they seated themselves to listen, and then proceeded to tell his story.

"I am Abraham's servant," he said. "The Lord has blessed my master abundantly, and he has become wealthy. He has given him sheep and cattle, silver and gold, menservants and maidservants, and camels and donkeys. My master's wife Sarah has borne him a son in her old age, and he has given him everything he owns. And my master made me swear an oath, and said, ' You must not get a wife for my son from the daughters of the Canaanites, in whose land I live, but go to my father's family and to my own clan, and get a wife for my son.'"

Rebekah listening fascinated, suddenly found her heart beating a little faster. She knew now what business this man had with her father. Abraham had sent him to find a wife for his son! She listened enraptured as the servant continued.

"When I came to the spring today, I said, 'O Lord, God of my master Abraham, if you will, please grant success to the journey on which I have come. See, I am standing beside this spring; if a maiden comes out to draw water and I say to her, "Please let me drink a little water from your jar," and if she says to me, "Drink, and I will draw water for your camels too," let her be the one the Lord has chosen for my master's son.'"

Rebekah's hand rose to her mouth. She could scarcely believe what she was hearing. She was the answer to this man's prayer! The Lord had led this man to her, and God had chosen her to be the wife of Abraham's son! Her eyes filled with sudden tears.

The servant was continuing his account and she listened spellbound.

"Before I finished praying in my heart, Rebekah came out, with her jar on her shoulder. She went down to the spring and drew water, and I said to her, 'Please give me a drink.' She quickly lowered her jar from her shoulder and said, 'Drink, and I will water your camels too.' So I drank, and she watered the camels also. I asked her, 'Whose daughter are you?'

"She said, 'The daughter of Bethuel son of Nahor, whom Milcah bore to him.'"

As she heard Abraham's devoted and godly servant bring his story to an end she felt like praising God along with him.

"I praised the Lord, the God of my master Abraham," the servant concluded, "who has led me on the right road to get the granddaughter of my master's brother for his son. Now if you will show kindness and faithfulness to my master, tell me; and if not, tell me, so that I may know which way to turn."

Rebekah held her breath. Then she heard her father give his answer, endorsed by her brother.

"This is from the Lord; we can say nothing to you one way or the other. Here is Rebekah; take her and go, and let her become the wife of your master's son, as the Lord has directed."

"I am going to be married!" Rebekah almost shouted, struggling between laughter and tears.

It was so amazing, so unexpected, so clearly from the Lord! Who would have thought this morning when she awakened that the day's end would bring such a remarkable change to her life?

She watched as the servant bowed to the ground before the Lord, grateful that the Lord had granted him a successful journey. He had come in search of a wife for Abraham's son, and Rebekah was thrilled that the Lord had chosen her. She also bowed her head in thanksgiving.

More gifts were handed out, wedding gifts of gold and silver jewellery and beautiful clothes. Rebekah was overwhelmed. She felt blessed indeed! Clearly she was going to marry a very wealthy man. Her mother and brother too received costly gifts of gold and silver, and there was great excitement in the family.

At last, his duty discharged, Abraham's servant and his men ate and drank and then retired to rest leaving the family to talk over the events of the day.

"I do not think I will be able to sleep tonight," sighed Rebekah happily.

She sat with her hands clasped around her knees, her eyes dreamy, her heart full. She wondered what Isaac looked like. To leave her family behind and marry a man she had not yet met was a little daunting, but she was certain it was what God had planned for her and she was content. She wanted to marry, and of course she wanted to have children, but she never imagined it would happen so suddenly and unexpectedly.

Morning came, and Rebekah, who had slept well after all, was dismayed to hear that Abraham's servant wanted to leave right away.

"Send me on my way to my master," he said.

Her mother and brother at once remonstrated.

"Let the girl remain with us ten days or so; then you may go," they pleaded.

But the servant replied, "Do not detain me, now that the Lord has granted success to my journey. Send me on my way so that I may go to my master."

Rebekah's mother and brother looked at each other.

"Let us call the girl and ask her about it," they suggested.

Rebekah, guessing that she was going to have to face separation from her family sooner than she had anticipated, came at once.

"Will you go with this man?" they asked.

Rebekah did not hesitate. "I will go," she said simply.

Then followed a rush to pack her belongings and get ready. Her beloved nurse and her maids were going with her, but at last they were all standing outside ready to leave, and the final goodbyes had to be said.

Her family gathered around her to give her their blessing.

"Our sister, may you increase to thousands upon thousands; may your offspring possess the gates of their enemies."

With a final embrace for her mother Rebekah mounted her camel, and with a last wave she followed

Abraham's servant and departed from her home in Haran.

Would she ever see it again? It was unlikely, she thought with a sigh. But ahead was a great adventure, and although she was sad to leave her family, she was looking forward to her new life in the land of God's promise as the wife of Isaac.

Days of weary travel followed, but one evening towards sunset the servant announced that they were within sight of their destination. A few minutes later Rebekah looked up and saw a man walking in the field. Suddenly nervous, she dismounted from her camel. If he was who she thought he was it would be more appropriate if she met him on the ground.

"Who is that man in the field coming to meet us?" she asked.

"He is my master," the servant answered.

Rebekah covered herself with a veil as they approached Isaac. She did not wish his immediate scrutiny until the servant had time to give his account, and explain who he had brought to him to be his wife. She felt it would detract from the charm of their meeting if he saw her first before he knew anything about her.

Isaac greeted his servant and acknowledged Rebekah's presence courteously. She stole a quick glance at him and was pleased to see that he was both handsome and kind looking..

It was only a short walk to the settlement where Isaac immediately gave orders for food and water to be brought for Rebekah and her maids. He brought Rebekah to his mother's tent and left her in the charge of his maidservants while he took his servant aside so that he could hear all he had to tell him.

Isaac's maidservants bathed Rebekah's feet, brought her some delicious food and helped her to change into a beautiful garment. She was ready to meet Isaac.

When he came in he stopped on the threshold as she rose to meet him. Slowly he came towards her, a smile on his lips, a tender look in his eyes.

"Rebekah," he said, taking her hands in his. "I did not know you would be so lovely. You are beautiful."

Rebekah raised her eyes to his and smiled. She felt her heart lurch. Their meeting was as perfect as she had hoped.

"My servant tells me you were exceedingly kind to him," continued Isaac, his voice quiet and gentle.

"I was happy to be of service to him," smiled Rebekah.

She felt very much at ease with this kind and courteous man.

"You have shown great kindness to me too," he said gently, "in coming with him to be my wife."

Again Rebekah smiled.

"I hope you will sleep well tonight," Isaac said. "This is my mother's tent. I miss her greatly, but now I will have you, and you will be a comfort to me."

"Yes," said Rebekah softly.

"Tomorrow we will be married," smiled Isaac. "Goodnight Rebekah."

As he was leaving he turned towards her again.

"I love you Rebekah," he said.

Chapter 13

"Are you all right Rebekah?" Isaac asked anxiously.

"I am not sure," replied Rebekah slowly. "Something strange is happening to me. I am a little afraid Isaac. We have waited so long for this baby."

"Twenty years," sighed Isaac. "It is a long time, but God has finally answered our prayers Rebekah. He has shown His kindness to us."

"Yes," nodded Rebekah. "But why is this happening to me? It feels as if a struggle is going on within me. This baby jumps and kicks such a lot, and I worry that there is something wrong."

She closed her eyes against the pain. When the discomfort eased she leaned back weakly against Isaac's shoulder.

"I will enquire of the Lord concerning this," she decided.

Later, in the cool of the day, she found her way to the altar that had been built long ago by Abraham. There in the sacred place of prayer and worship she poured out her heart before the Lord. Quietly, tearfully, and expectantly she waited to hear what He would say to her.

"Two nations are in your womb," the Lord told her, "and two peoples from within you will be separated; one people will be stronger that the other, and the older will serve the younger."

"Two babies instead of just one!" Rebekah exclaimed incredulously. "Isaac will be delighted."

Rebekah rose to her feet, her prayers and thanksgiving complete.

"Two nations, two peoples," she mused as she returned to the tent. "And the older will serve the younger. That means the younger will be the more important of the two. He will receive the blessing of the firstborn, even though he is not the firstborn."

Isaac's face lit up when she told him what the Lord had said.

"Two sons, two nations, two peoples!" he said excitedly, just as Rebekah had done. "God is fulfilling His promise. He revealed to my father that his descendants would be as numerous as the stars in the sky. He promised that He would bless my mother so that she would be the mother of nations. I am their only child Rebekah, but now God is giving us two sons who will become two separate peoples."

"I feel so privileged to be part of God's plan," Rebekah said happily.

"I know," said Isaac softly, putting his arms around Rebekah and holding her close. "I love you Rebekah. Please take good care of yourself while you are carrying these babies."

"I will," promised Rebekah.

Later when she told Deborah, her nurse that she was expecting two babies, Deborah too advised her to look after herself.

"You will need all your strength to deliver two of them," she warned, "so you must be careful."

Rebekah, always active and energetic found it hard to rest, but at length the long and uneventful days of her confinement were over and the babies were ready to be born into the world.

The first to appear was red all over and his little body was covered in fine downy hair. Very quickly after him came the second baby, and strangely his tiny hand was grasping the heel of his brother.

Her birth pangs over, Rebekah smiled delightedly as Deborah placed the babies in her arms. She gazed at them lovingly as she held them.

"We will call this one Esau," she laughed, looking up at Deborah. "It is a fitting name because of his colour and the hair on his body."

Turning to her second baby boy she looked at him closely, remembering what the Lord had told her about the younger twin.

"Jacob is a good name for you," she smiled, kissing him gently. "You desperately wanted to be the firstborn, so you were trying to hold your brother back. Never mind, you will be the more important one when you are grown up. God has spoken to me about you, and I will tell you all about it some day."

"They are two healthy little boys," Deborah told her cheerfully.

"Yes," said Rebekah. "I am so thankful to God. Deborah, please tell Isaac to come and see his two beautiful sons."

Chapter 14

"My sons are so very different from each other," mused Rebekah.

She hated to have to admit it, even to herself, but Jacob was her favourite.

"He is quiet and diligent and he has never given me any cause for anxiety."

As the boys had grown into manhood their characters had developed in totally different directions. In many ways, to Rebekah at least, it was no surprise that Esau had grown up to be a rugged outdoor man determined to live life to the full in the physical realm. His appearance at birth had hinted at this.

"He is strong and masculine," said Isaac proudly, "so naturally he loves to engage in physical activity, and he enjoys the open countryside."

"But he has no interest in our God, the God of our fathers," ventured Rebekah. "Those pagan girls he has married are a source of great grief to me."

Isaac sighed. "Yes, they are a grief to me too," he admitted. "He should have chosen more carefully, but he is impulsive by nature."

"All he cares about is his hunting," Rebekah complained.

"He has become very skilled in it," countered Isaac. "He loves the thrill of the chase. You can see how his eyes shine with excitement when he comes in from the fields, and I must say I greatly enjoy the rich venison he provides."

"Yes, I know," said Rebekah, "and I would not deny him that pleasure, but has he any interest in matters of the soul? It seems to me he is more interested in sensual gratification than in anything spiritual."

"He is still young," defended Isaac. "He will settle down."

"Jacob is more spiritual," suggested Rebekah. "He cares about the promise handed down from Abraham to you Isaac. It pains me to think that Esau will not take it seriously if it is handed down to him."

"He will change when he has to," Isaac said firmly. "The blessing of the birthright belongs to him Rebekah. He has to take it seriously."

Rebekah said nothing more, but she could not help contrasting her two sons: Esau; brash, impetuous, worldly, while Jacob was quiet, considerate, and respectful.

Isaac did not appear to accept that Esau's character was unsuited to the spiritual responsibilities that came with the birthright. God had made gracious promises to Abraham which had passed down to Isaac who would in turn pass them on to his son.

"I will make you into a great nation, and I will bless you .... and all peoples on earth will be blessed through you," God had told Abraham.

God had repeated His promises to Isaac telling him, "I will make your descendants as numerous as the stars in the sky, and will give them all these lands, and through your offspring all nations on earth will be blessed because Abraham obeyed Me and kept My requirements, My commands, My decrees and My laws."

It was incumbent upon Isaac's son as inheritor of God's promises, to obey God and keep alive the spiritual tradition handed down from father to son. Would Esau maintain the firm belief in God and His promises that was needed to fulfil the terms of the birthright blessing?

"I cannot see Esau doing this," worried Rebekah, "but I believe Jacob would."

Rebekah had always been closer to Jacob. He never strayed far from home, preferring a quiet, simple domestic life keeping flocks and growing vegetables. Not for him the excitement of the hunt or the killing of animals. He was respectful and obedient to his parents, taking an interest in the spiritual matters which were so important to them. God had revealed to her before the boys were born that the elder would serve the younger, and Rebekah knew that God had chosen Jacob to receive the birthright usually reserved for the eldest son.

"How can I make Isaac see this?" pondered Rebekah.

Isaac was ageing, and Rebekah could see that when it came to passing on the birthright Isaac's sights were firmly set on Esau. He was proud of his prowess as a hunter, he admired his physical strength, and he had a taste for the game Esau brought to his table.

Furthermore, he was the eldest son, so for Isaac the matter was settled.

"Isaac thinks he will change when he is faced with his responsibilities," thought Rebekah, "but I know him, and he has no interest in living a godly life, whereas Jacob wants to know God. I can see that he desires to know Him."

She sighed deeply. In addition to the revelation God had given her, she knew with a mother's intuition, that Jacob was the one who should inherit the birthright with its promised blessings, and perpetuate the faith of his father to succeeding generations.

"I will just have to find a way to make it happen," she said decidedly.

Chapter 15

As Rebekah listened to the conversation between her husband and Esau she knew that the time she was dreading had come.

"I am now an old man and do not know the day of my death," Isaac told Esau. "Now then, get your weapons—your quiver and bow—and go out to the open country to hunt some wild game for me. Prepare me the kind of tasty food I like and bring it to me to eat, so that I may give you my blessing before I die."

As Esau left to hunt game for his father, Rebekah reflected that Isaac had been a good husband over their long marriage, but he had reached old age, his strength had diminished and his eyesight had gone. It was time to pass on the birthright blessing.

"I just do not want it to go to Esau," muttered Rebekah to herself. "Jacob is the one who should receive it. God told me so before they were born. This is the one subject upon which Isaac and I have disagreed."

As she went to find Jacob she was formulating a plan in her mind to ensure that what God had decreed would come to pass. It was time for her to act.

"Jacob," she said as soon as she reached him, "I overheard your father say to your brother Esau, 'Bring me some game and prepare me some tasty food, so that I may give you my blessing in the presence of the Lord before I die.'

"Now my son, listen carefully and do what I tell you. Go out to the flock and bring me two choice young goats, so that I can prepare some tasty food for your father, just the way he likes it. Then take it to your father to eat, so that he may give you his blessing before he dies."

Unlike his impulsive brother Jacob never rushed into anything so he hesitated.

"But my brother Esau is a hairy man, and I am a man with smooth skin", he remonstrated. "What if my father touches me? I would appear to be tricking him and would bring down a curse on myself rather than a blessing."

"My son, let the curse fall on me," Rebekah said bravely and decidedly. "Just do what I say; go and get them for me."

Still looking apprehensive, Jacob left to do his mother's bidding. When he returned she immediately set about preparing the goat stew the way she knew Isaac liked it.

"Now for the difficult part," thought Rebekah.

She hated to deceive her beloved Isaac, but the end justified the means. She could see no other way.

She had kept in her possession some of Esau's best clothes which she now gave to Jacob to put on. Cleverly she arranged the goat skins over his hands and neck so that if his father touched him Jacob would feel hairy like Esau. She knew Jacob was nervous but also keen to receive the birthright blessing, so she handed him the tasty stew and bread she had made and pushed him in the direction of his father, while she listened out of sight.

"Who is it?" she heard Isaac say.

"I am Esau your firstborn. I have done as you told me. Please sit up and eat some of my game so that you may give me your blessing."

"How did you find it so quickly, my son?" asked Isaac.

"The Lord your God gave me success," Jacob replied.

Then Isaac said to Jacob, "Come near so I can touch you, my son, to know whether you really are my son Esau or not."

Rebekah hardly dared to breathe. Would the disguise work or would Isaac know it was not Esau?

"The voice is the voice of Jacob, but the hands are the hands of Esau," Isaac said.

Rebekah let her breath out slowly. Her heart was pounding.

"Are you really my son Esau?" he persisted.

"I am," Jacob replied.

Isaac seemed satisfied, so he said the words that Rebekah longed to hear him say.

"My son, bring me some of your game to eat, so that I may give you my blessing."

Relief flooded over Rebekah as Isaac ate the food which Jacob offered him. As Jacob bent to kiss his father, Isaac must have caught the smell of Esau from his clothes, and finally, completely convinced, he spoke as if to Esau.

"Ah, the smell of my son is like the smell of a field that the Lord has blessed."

Then he pronounced his blessing.

"May God give you of heaven's dew and of earth's richness–an abundance of grain and new wine. May nations serve you and peoples bow down to you. Be lord over your brothers, and may the sons of your mother bow down to you. May those who curse you be cursed and those who bless you be blessed."

Rebekah had heard enough and she slipped away. She had done the right thing for Jacob, but what would happen when Esau returned? She found herself trembling, both from fear and from the emotion of what had just taken place. She had encouraged her son to deceive his father, and for that she felt great guilt, but she had to make God's declaration come true. It was up to her, was it not?

She heard Esau return and go to his father, but this time she did not listen. Esau would be furious and disappointed, but he would get over it in due course. He would continue to hunt game and follow his outdoor pursuits, and forget that Jacob had stolen his birthright. Careless and indifferent regarding the spiritual responsibilities that came with the birthright he would not regret that this aspect was denied to him, but he would be angry that all his father's wealth would not pass to him. Still, he was skilled with his quiver and bow and he could do well for himself.

It was not long before Rebekah discovered just how angry Esau was. One of her servants came with news.

"I heard Esau say, 'The days of mourning for my father are near; then I will kill my brother Jacob.'"

Alarmed, Rebekah sent for Jacob immediately.

"Your brother Esau is consoling himself with the thought of killing you. Now then, my son, do what I say: Flee at once to my brother Laban in Haran. Stay with him for a while until your brother's fury subsides. When your brother is no longer angry with you and forgets what you did to him, I will send word for you to come back from there. Why should I lose both of you in one day?"

Much as she disliked sending Jacob away she believed it was the only way to preserve his life. Esau was quick tempered and Rebekah was afraid that he would take his revenge on Jacob at the first opportunity. She did not believe he would hold a grudge for ever, but while he raged and threatened it was best to have Jacob leave. The ideal place would be with her family, and she knew how to talk Isaac around.

"Isaac," she said. "I am tired of living because of these Hittite women. If Jacob takes a wife from among the women of this land, from Hittite women like these, my life will not be worth living."

"Very well," agreed Isaac. "I will send for Jacob and tell him what he must do."

Rebekah smiled a little at her success, but she knew it meant that Jacob would be leaving immediately and that saddened her greatly. She would miss him so much.

"Do not marry a Canaanite woman," instructed Isaac when Jacob arrived. "Go at once to Paddan Aram, to the house of your mother's father Bethuel. Take a wife for yourself there, from among the daughters of Laban, your mother's brother. May God Almighty bless you and make you fruitful and increase your numbers until you become a community of peoples. May He give you and your descendants the blessing given to Abraham, so that you may take possession of the land where you now live as an alien, the land God gave to Abraham."

As Rebekah listened to Isaac's gracious words of blessing to Jacob, she felt deeply moved. God's promise was now invested in Jacob. He would inherit the blessing passed down from his father and grandfather. One day his descendants would inhabit the land God promised Abraham, and become as numerous as the stars in the sky. Abraham, Isaac, and now Jacob! He was part of God's plan. She had given him birth, she had ensured he received the birthright blessing. Now she had to let him go.

"Good-bye dear Jacob. May God go with you and bless you, and be your God."

Chapter 16

"**J**ust because you are my relative, should you work for me for nothing? Tell me what your wages should be."

Leah, listening from a respectable distance waited with interest for his answer.

Since their cousin from the west had arrived they had all enjoyed the break from the monotony of life when the only eventful happening of the day was meeting the shepherds at the well, and removing the stone to water the sheep.

Leah had not seen much of him over the few weeks he had been here. He had been out in the fields with Rachel and the servants most days, helping with the sheep. Leah had watched enviously as her beautiful sister with her youthful vivacity and robust health had gone out to tend her flocks each day with Jacob to keep her company.

Jacob was answering her father and Leah leaned closer to hear.

"I will work for you for seven years for your younger daughter Rachel."

Leah gasped. Hurriedly she moved out of earshot, into the cool air of evening.

"I am the eldest!" she burst out. "It is not fair. Why should he ask for Rachel? He should be asking for me."

When she regained her composure she acknowledged that it was only natural that a man would be more attracted to her lovely sister. Rachel was exquisite in face and form, full of life and vitality, while she herself was plain and dull.

"I wish I was like her," she thought wistfully.

She could not stand up to the rigours of sheep farming where the flock had to be moved from field to pasture and brought back for watering in the evening. The watering pots were heavy and it took a long time, for her father had many flocks of sheep and goats. Rachel seemed to exult in her occupation as a shepherdess, and she loved the freedom of outdoor life, rising at dawn each day and returning at sunset, her face glowing with radiance and health.

"I envy her," said Leah fiercely. "She has beauty, vivacity and charm. I have none of those qualities. Naturally Jacob would fall in love with her. Besides he met her first at the well when he arrived. I had no chance."

She sighed and tried to blink back her tears.

"Father will give his consent, and they will be married and I will be left."

It was not a happy outlook. Leah knew she was not beautiful. She was pale, without the glowing colour in her cheeks which Rachel had, her eyes were weak, so unlike Rachel's with their vibrant sparkle, and she was not graceful like her sister.

"It is not fair," she muttered again.

It was humiliating that her younger sister would be married before her.

"Will I ever have the chance to be married at all?" wondered Leah.

It did not seem likely. Her family was the only family in Haran who were worshippers of Yahwey, and while her father was not overly devoted to his God, he would not marry his daughter to a pagan. Nor would Leah wish it. She had grown up in the traditions of the believing community and had always been faithful to her God.

Seven years! The marriage was a long way off. Meanwhile she would have to live each day knowing that Rachel was betrothed to Jacob, and that they would be married one day, while she would be left desolate. Unless a suitable man could be found she would have to remain unmarried and childless.

"Is it possible that someone might come into my life just as Jacob came into Rachel's?" she wondered.

There was always that hope!

Chapter 17

even years had passed since Jacob had asked for Rachel's hand in marriage. Now the day of their wedding had come.

Jacob had been heard to say that the seven years had seemed like only a few days to him because of his love for her.

"How blessed she is!" thought Leah. "I wish someone would love me like that."

If the seven years had seemed short to Jacob, they had seemed long to Leah. In all that time no other suitor had come forward as a husband for her, and there did not seem any likelihood of it ever happening.

"How will I bear it?" Leah wondered sadly.

She could see the long years stretching ahead with Rachel and Jacob happily married and babies being born to them, while she would languish alone and unloved, and never have the chance to hold a child of her own in her arms.

Her father had brought the people of the neighbourhood together along with the family to celebrate this important event, and there was an abundance of food and wine for the guests, but Leah did not feel like joining in the celebrations. She wandered aimlessly around, not wanting to talk to anyone.

She could see that Jacob was enjoying himself among a group of men, as well he might. He had waited long and worked hard for Rachel, and now that she was about to become his wife he had every reason to be joyful.

"I am the only one who is not happy," thought Leah, a little guiltily. She ought to be happy for her sister, but life seemed unfair, and she could not summon up any joy on this occasion.

The sun was at last beginning to sink westward, and soon it would be dark. Leah felt she would be glad to see night come when this day would be ended.

"Leah!"

Her mother's voice made her jump, so engrossed had she been in her own thoughts.

"Leah, I have been looking for you everywhere. Your father wishes to speak with you."

"Yes mother, I will go at once," she replied.

"I will come with you," said her mother, taking her arm.

As she entered her father's house, Laban stood up and took her by the hand.

"Leah, I am giving you to Jacob," he said, coming straight to the point. "It is not right that Rachel should be married before you."

Leah gasped.

"But …Rachel … what …"

"Do not worry about Rachel," her father interrupted. "I have it all under control."

"But …but…What about Jacob? What will he say when …?"

Her father laughed, heartlessly, Leah thought.

"Leave him to me. Just do as I say, my daughter. Go with your mother now and get dressed for the ceremony."

Stunned, unbelieving, almost daring to taste happiness, yet filled with apprehension, Leah allowed her mother to take her by the hand and lead her to her room.

"Mother, what will Jacob say? You know it is Rachel he wants."

"Just do as your father says Leah," her mother said kindly.

"But I am afraid Mother. What will Jacob say when he finds it is me and not Rachel?"

Her mother smiled wryly.

"He is well into his wine," she said. "He will not notice."

"Maybe not tonight ... but in the morning." Leah could not bring herself to say more.

"By that time it will be too late," her mother said gently. "You will be his wife, and he will have to accept it."

"I will be his wife," repeated Leah, momentarily happy.

Leah's emotions were in turmoil as she permitted her mother to help her into the beautiful gown that had been meant for Rachel. Her mother placed a veil over her face.

"He will not know that it is you Leah. Do not be afraid." she whispered.

"Where is Rachel?" Leah asked suddenly.

"Your father has left her in the care of her maids. She will be upset of course, but she is young ...and ..." her voice faltered.

"And beautiful," finished Leah, "and I am not."

"You are a good girl Leah, and you will make him a good wife. May God grant you many sons," she said, kissing Leah tenderly.

Her father was at the door.

"Take my arm Leah, and come with me," he said firmly.

Happiness and fear struggled together in Leah's heart as she walked beside her father. Pity too, stirred within her, for Jacob and for Rachel. What her father was doing was unfair to them, but he had made this decision and his word had to be obeyed.

Jacob arose as they arrived, and quietness descended over the wedding guests. Leah took a quick glance at Jacob. He looked so happy. Could she do this to him? But it was her chance for happiness. Besides, she dare not disobey her father. A moment longer and she was ready.

Laban placed Leah's hand in Jacob's and spoke the blessing that made them husband and wife.

With her hand still in his Leah walked quietly alongside Jacob to his tent.

Chapter 18

*I*t was morning. Jacob lay sleeping beside her, but Leah had been awake for a long time. The sun was just rising and light was beginning to filter into the tent.

Leah gazed at the man who was now her husband, and again felt a stab of pity for him and for Rachel.

Once more happiness and fear alternatively gripped her as she lay there waiting for Jacob to awaken. On the one hand she felt regret that Jacob had been so cruelly duped, but she could not help feeling elated on her own account. Her father had given her a wonderful gift, the blessing of marriage. Whatever happened when Jacob awoke, nothing could take that away from her.

Jacob was stirring, and Leah's heart began to pound. Nervously she watched him as he stretched and slowly opened his eyes.

Turning towards her with a smile on his lips he murmured, "Rachel."

The name was scarcely uttered when his eyes fell on Leah, and he started back with shock, the colour draining from his face.

"Leah!"

"You … you must speak to my father," stammered Leah faintly.

Without saying another word, Jacob dressed quickly and went out. Hastily Leah put on her clothes and followed. She wanted to hear what her father would have to say to his nephew whom he had so wronged.

"What is this you have done to me?" demanded Jacob hotly. "I served you for Rachel, did I not? Why have you deceived me?"

Laban held up his hand as if to silence him.

"It is not our custom here to give the younger daughter in marriage before the older one," he said cooly. "Finish this daughter's bridal week; then we will give you the younger one also, in return for another seven years of work."

Jacob stared at him long and hard, his expression changing from fury to shock to disbelief, but in the end there was nothing he could do but agree. He simply nodded and turned away. Leah caught her father's triumphant smile as Jacob strode off. He was not a man who engaged in confrontation and Laban knew it.

Leah did not follow him, but went in search of her mother.

"He is hurt and angry Mother, as I knew he would be."

Then with a sudden realisation of her own position in view of what her father had just told Jacob, she poured out her own hurt, anger and dismay.

"I am going to have to share him with Rachel," she cried, staring wide-eyed at her mother. "And it is her he loves. He does not care for me."

She laid her head on her mother's lap and wept bitter tears of disappointment.

Her mother stroked her hair gently. Gradually Leah's sobbing subsided and she looked up.

"How did Rachel take it last night?" she asked.

"She was angry and upset, but now that she knows she too will marry Jacob she is more cheerful. You will both have to be content with the situation as it is," her mother advised.

"Yes, I suppose so," conceded Leah.

She still felt uneasy. It was far from ideal. She was Jacob's wife, but there was no denying it was Rachel he loved, and once she became his wife too, he would spend all of his time with her.

"I just hope I can give him a child," thought Leah. "That way he will become more attached to me."

The days passed, and at the end of her bridal week, Leah, as she had predicted, was left on her own, as Jacob and Rachel were wrapped up in each other.

But as days turned into weeks life began to take a better turn for Leah. She told her mother first.

"I am with child, Mother," she announced excitedly. "Now perhaps Jacob will love me, at least a little."

"It will make him very happy," her mother said, hugging her. "You had better go and tell him Leah."

Chapter 19

or the first time in her marriage Leah tasted happiness. She had just given birth to a healthy baby boy, and as she gazed tenderly at her little son she thrilled to the joy of motherhood, a blessing she once thought she would never know.

She named him Reuben, which adequately expressed her feelings, for it meant "see, a son!" It was a small victory for her in the marriage where she was the unloved wife, while her sister was the adored and cherished woman who was the love of Jacob's life.

"It is because the Lord has seen my misery. Surely my husband will love me now," she said.

Alas, this did not happen, and when her second son was born she said, "Because the Lord has heard that I am not loved, He gave me this one too."

She called him Simeon which affirmed her belief in "the One who hears."

A third son followed in due course, and this time Leah voiced her hope that their three sons would draw Jacob into a closer relationship with her as his wife and the mother of his children.

"Now at last my husband will become attached to me because I have borne him three sons," she said, so she named him Levi, which meant "attached".

Much to her disappointment she could see that Jacob was still very much more attached to Rachel than he was to her. She despaired that he would ever care for her.

When her fourth son came along she named him Judah, saying simply, "This time I will praise the Lord."

Although her prayers had not been answered in the way she had hoped, Leah knew that God had seen her distress, and He had not left her desolate. He had given her four healthy children and she was now able to praise Him. Perhaps this fourth son, whose name meant 'praise', would be specially blessed by God because, she, his mother, had chosen to praise God for the blessings He had given her instead of always complaining about what she did not have.

In all this time Rachel, who spent more time with Jacob than she did, still had no children, and Leah knew she was desperate, so desperate in fact that she had a quarrel with Jacob, and subsequently gave him her maid Bilhah in the hope that she could build a family through her.

When Bilhah gave birth to a son, Rachel named him Dan, and declared, "God has vindicated me; He has listened to my plea and given me a son."

A second son born to Bilhah caused Rachel to proclaim, "I have had a great struggle with my sister, and I have won." She named him Naphtali.

There was open hostility between the sisters now. Leah knew that Rachel was envious of her because she had given Jacob four sons, and she admitted to herself that she was jealous of Rachel because of Jacob's love for her.

"I have four sons but I am not loved," she said sadly.

In her innermost being love was what Leah longed for. Thinking about it, she realised that of the two men in her life, not even her father cared about her. He had placed her in an intolerable position for his own ends. He wanted to keep Jacob in his service for another seven years, and he had neatly managed to trade off his two daughters in order to accomplish this. She reflected, as she had done many times before, that it had been unfair to both of them as well as Jacob.

"If I was Jacob's only wife he would learn to love me, especially after giving him four sons," she said to herself.

Even as she said it she knew instinctively that this was not true. Jacob's love for Rachel was intense, and he was the kind of man who loved deeply. He was not capable of loving another.

She had watched Jacob and Rachel together, and it was evident that they only had eyes for each other. Leah knew now that Jacob's love would never be hers, but she had her precious children while Rachel had none. That would have to suffice.

"And it does, most of the time," acknowledged Leah.

When it became clear that Rachel was building a family through Bilhah, Leah feared Rachel might overtake her her in the number of children she acquired, so she decided to give her maid Zilpah to Jacob, so that she could have more children through her.

Accordingly Zilpah gave birth to a baby boy whom Leah named Gad.

"What good fortune!" she exclaimed.

Later another son was born to Zilpah, and Leah named him Asher.

"How happy I am!" she smiled. "The women will call me happy."

Six sons! Four of her own, and two by Zilpah, while Rachel only had two by her maid and none of her own.

"I am prevailing over my sister," thought Leah gleefully.

But the old bitterness over her loveless marriage still existed as she was to discover over the incident of the mandrakes.

It was wheat harvest and Leah had scarcely seen Jacob for months. He was constantly occupied in Laban's service, and when he came home he spent the nights with Rachel.

One day little Reuben, her firstborn, brought her some mandrakes which he found in the field. Rachel, who happened to be passing when the little boy arrived, caught sight of the mandrakes and her eyes lit up.

"Please give me some of your son's mandrakes," she requested.

Leah knew why she asked. The mandrakes were believed to induce fertility, so she could see why Rachel wanted them, but in a sudden unreasonable burst of anger against her sister Leah was ungracious in her reply.

"Was it not enough that you took away my husband?" she snapped. "Will you take my son's mandrakes too?"

"Very well," Rachel said. "He can sleep with you tonight in return for your son's mandrakes."

This was an unexpected outcome and Leah was exultant. She could hardly wait to see Jacob, and as soon as he came in from the fields that night she ran to meet him.

"You must sleep with me tonight," she told him triumphantly. "I have hired you with my son's mandrakes."

Not long afterwards she was delighted to discover that she was pregnant again.

When her fifth son arrived she named him Issachar.

"God has rewarded me for giving my maidservant to my husband," she declared.

Five sons entitled Leah to some marital rights, and in the course of time a sixth son was born to her.

She named him Zebulun and announced happily, "God has presented me with a precious gift. This time my husband will treat me with honour, because I have borne him six sons."

God had been good to her and gratefully Leah acknowledged it. In spite of the adversity of her situation God had been giving her precious gifts. Six sons! How blessed she was!. And Jacob did honour her even if he did not love her.

One more beautiful gift came her way in the form of a lovely little daughter.

"I am blessed indeed," Leah smiled. "I will call her Dinah."

Seven children! Even if she lacked a husband's love, she had seven reasons to be thankful.

Chapter 20

*L*eah was surprised to receive a message from Jacob telling her that she and Rachel should meet him at once in the fields where he was working. This was unusual. He had never made such a request before, and as she hurried out to him along with her sister, Leah wondered what the reason could be for this urgent summons.

When they reached him Jacob drew them aside out of earshot of the servants.

"I see that your father's attitude towards me is not what it was before," he began. "But the God of my father has been with me. You know that I have worked for your father with all my strength, yet your father has cheated me by changing my wages ten times. However God has not allowed him to harm me."

Leah, along with her sister, listened with growing indignation as Jacob described how their father had treated him, trying to deny him the opportunity of building up a flock for himself which was his due wages, and attempting to deprive him of the strongest animals, leaving him the weakest of the flocks. But God had prospered him despite this, and he had gained large healthy flocks while Laban's flocks diminished.

Jacob concluded his account by telling them that the angel of God had spoken to him in a dream, and that God had seen all that Laban was doing to him.

"God spoke to me," he told them. "He said, 'I am the God of Bethel, where you anointed a pillar and where you made a vow to me. Now leave this land at once and go back to your native land.'"

Leah looked at Rachel and they both turned back to Jacob.

"Do we still have any share in the inheritance of our father's estate?" they said angrily. "Does he not regard us as foreigners? Not only has he sold us, but he has used up what was paid for us. Surely all the wealth that God took away from our father belongs to us and our children. So do whatever God has told you."

A few more minutes were spent discussing arrangements for their departure, then Leah left quickly to gather her children together.

"Reuben, Simeon, Levi, Judah, Issachar, Zebulun, and baby Dinah. My seven lovely children! Now my children we are going on a long journey."

In addition there were Zilpah's two sons, Bilhah's two sons, and Rachel's little boy Joseph, for Rachel had finally given birth to a child of her own, much to the relief of the whole family.

Twelve children, an impressive retinue of servants, and large flocks of sheep, goats, camels and donkeys. It would be a mammoth undertaking.

"Jacob has become rich," thought Leah with satisfaction. "It is only right considering the way my father treated him, and how hard he has worked. The Lord has blessed him, He has blessed us all."

It was still early when they left Paddan Aram. Jacob had warned that they must leave secretly as he feared Laban would try to stop them, so they left without his knowledge. It was regrettable, since they could not say goodbye, but Leah knew Jacob was right. Her father would try to keep him. Jacob had served his uncle well, but now he wanted a life of his own back in the land of his birth.

"It is twenty years since Jacob arrived here with nothing," Leah reflected.

They had been difficult years, not just for Jacob, but for her, and for Rachel too, she grudgingly conceded. There had been good times as well, the births of the children especially. Now they were going to Canaan, the land God had promised to give to Jacob and his descendants.

They were encamped in the hill country of Gilead when Laban caught up with them and demanded to know why Jacob had run off secretly with his daughters and grandchildren.

"I was afraid," Jacob answered honestly, "because I thought you would take your daughters away from me by force."

Both Jacob and Laban said a great deal more before finally reaching an understanding. That evening they made a covenant between them, setting up stones as witness to their agreement. Leah was thankful that they would part amicably.

The following morning Laban kissed his daughters and grandchildren and gave them his blessing. Leah was glad that after all they were able to say goodbye.

As they continued their journey with their children, their flocks and their servants Leah realised that God's blessing had already come to pass in Jacob's life.

God had said, "May God Almighty bless you and make you fruitful and increase your numbers until you become a community of peoples."

"I am blessed to have had a part to play in that," said Leah with deep emotion.

"Jacob has eleven sons, six of them mine," she thought proudly. "

She looked at her children lovingly.

"Whatever lies ahead for my boys I know that they will be blessed by God. He has given His promise to Abraham, Isaac and Jacob, and He will continue to bless my sons and their descendants for future generations to come."

Chapter 21

" 𝓛 ive as a widow in your father's house until my son Shelah grows up," Judah had told her.

Young as she was, Tamar had known great tragedy. Twice widowed, and childless, she was now desolate in her father's house, compelled to wait until the youngest son of her father-in-law was old enough to marry.

"I am glad this is a custom in Judah's family," she thought, "even though I must wait until Shelah grows up. I want to be part of this family."

In the Canaanite region of Adullam where she lived, Tamar's family and all their neighbours worshipped many gods. Not so Judah's family. They worshipped only one God whom they called Yahwey.

"I like the idea of only one God," Tamar had said when she married Er, the eldest of Judah's three sons.

Sadly, Er had not cared about Yahwey. Tamar grew sombre as she reflected on his indifference towards his God. Perhaps it was because his mother was a Canaanite. Perhaps his father, though a God-worshipper, had not encouraged him to follow in the family tradition.

"Why, if you have such an amazing God as Yahwey, would you not want to worship Him?" Tamar had questioned.

It seemed to her that this God was worth worship-ping. Judah's ancestors had all been devout worship-pers of Yahwey, and He had blessed them abundantly and had promised great blessings to their descendants. They would eventually own the land where they dwelt, and they would have numerous offspring from whom would come kings and nations.

"I want to be part of that," declared Tamar decisively.

Her thoughts turned back to the time she had first met Judah when he had sought her as a wife for his firstborn. Her family knew of him through his friend Hirah who was an Adullamite, and so they had been agreeable to the marriage. Judah was one of twelve brothers, and his father Jacob was devoted to his God.

Jacob was immensely rich because God had blessed him, and he was well respected among the Canaanites.

"I was so happy to marry into their family," remembered Tamar, "because I liked what I heard of their God."

Tamar had not been married long when she suddenly found herself widowed. After she had grieved for Er she was given in marriage to Onan, Judah's second son, in accordance with the tradition of Judah's family. She wept afresh as she recalled the humiliation she had endured as Onan's wife. He refused to fulfil his duty to her as Er's widow so that she could have a child to honour her first husband and leave an heir to keep his name alive.

This marriage too was cut short by the death of Onan, who like his brother, had no respect for his God. Deeply shocked that these sons of Judah had shown such antipathy towards their God, Tamar determined that she would believe in Him and trust Him for a future in Judah's family.

Years passed. Tamar had been waiting a long time for Judah to fulfil his promise, too long, she thought. Shelah was now a young man of marriageable age, but Judah had not approached her to arrange a marriage with his youngest son. She could only conclude that he did not want her in the family.

"Perhaps in some way he blames me for the deaths of Er and Onan," she worried. "If he thinks that I still adhere to Canaanite gods he may not want to trust Shelah to me. Does he not know that I care more about his God that his sons did?"

Tamar longed to talk to Judah, to explain to him that she believed in his God, that she wanted to take her place in his family, that indeed she had a right to belong to his family, but he had cut off all communication with her.

"What can I do?" she wondered.

It seemed there was nothing she could do. She was helpless. Waiting was the only course left open to her.

"I will not give up," she said decidedly. "I will wait and hope."

Time passed. Then at last her chance came.

Judah's wife died, and in due course, after a period of grieving, Judah was ready to take up his everyday life once more.

It was sheep shearing season, a time of festivity and merriment. Traditionally families would get together to celebrate and invite their friends, and even their servants to a sumptuous feast.

Tamar was told, "Your father-in-law is on his way to Timnah to shear his sheep."

"What can I do?" wondered Tamar.

Tentatively she formed a plan in her mind, an outrageous, daring plan which, if it failed, would mean certain death for her.

"It is my only chance," she told herself.

She discarded her widow's clothes, dressed in bright colourful garments, and covered her face with a veil, hoping it would conceal her sufficiently. Bravely she left the safety of her home and sat down at the entrance to Emain which was on the road to Timnah. Nervously she waited for Judah to pass by. He would be in high spirits, she believed, as he anticipated the feasting and mirth.

When Judah sighted her he immediately approached her. At once he asked to engage her services, clearly believing her to be a prostitute.

"And what will you give me?" she asked, disguising her voice.

"I will send a young goat from my flock," Judah promised.

Tamar knew she must protect herself to ensure that Judah could not deny that he had been with her.

"Will you give me something as a pledge until you send it?" she asked cleverly.

Judah looked surprised but asked, "What pledge should I give you?"

"Your seal and its cord, and the staff in your hand," she answered.

She knew that in parting with these Judah would be left vulnerable, but he agreed, and satisfied, but still uneasy lest she be discovered, Tamar led him to a quiet place, and there she lay with him, hoping, longing, believing that she would become the mother of his child.

Tamar slipped away while Judah slept, returned hastily to her home, and donned her widow's clothes once more.

Soon, much to her great joy, Tamar knew she was pregnant.

"My plan has worked!" she thought with delight.

She hugged the discovery to herself. She would not tell anyone just yet. Her secret must wait a little longer. Soon enough it would become known and she would then have to put the next part of her plan into action.

Carefully she guarded Judah's seal and staff. When the time came they would be her lifeline. Tamar knew there was still an element of danger in her scheme, but in spite of Judah's broken promise to marry her to his third son, she felt he was still a man of integrity. He had given his pledge and he would honour it. When she produced his seal and staff he would have to admit they were his.

Three months passed and it was time to let it be known that she was with child. She knew word would reach Judah quickly and he would be told that his daughter-in-law was guilty of prostitution, and as a result she was pregnant. She would not have long to wait for his reaction.

"Bring her out and have her burned to death," ordered Judah furiously.

Tamar's heart beat painfully and her mouth was dry. She had already been found guilty and condemned. She knew there would be no mercy. Clutching Judah's seal and staff she struggled to keep her nerve as she was dragged outside.

"Take this message to my father-in-law," she gasped. "Tell him I am pregnant by the man who owns these."

She relinquished the precious items when she saw Judah among the crowd.

"See if you recognise whose seal and cord and staff these are," she shouted bravely.

For a moment she waited, breathless and trembling, her heart in her mouth. She watched as Judah's face registered recognition of his belongings, and after a moment's silence he spoke.

"She is more righteous than I, since I would not give her to my son Shelah."

Tamar almost fainted with relief. Weakly she leaned against the wall. Though her heart was beating wildly, she felt deep thankfulness within. Her determination and courage had gained her the result she so greatly desired. Now she would live in Judah's house as his rightful daughter-in-law, and she would give birth to the child she had so longed for, a child who would be a member of Judah's family, who would inherit the blessings of Judah's God.

"Bring her to my house," Judah instructed her family. "She has the right to my provision and protection."

The days of waiting in Judah's house were peaceful. As Tamar reflected on her desperate scheme to remain part of Judah's family she knew it had been worthwhile to go through with it.

Later when she held her twin boys in her arms she wept with joy and thankfulness.

"Perez and Zerah, my little sons, Judah's sons. You will grow up knowing Judah's God, my God. He is a God worth knowing."

Chapter 22

"*S*unrise never ceases to thrill me!" exclaimed Rahab.

One moment the night was black as pitch, the next moment darkness vanished and there was light; pale, cold, colourless light at first, but gradually, subtly, exquisitely the light changed and varied through a myriad different hues and tones as the red-gold outline of the rising sun took shape against a sky of palest azure. Night slipped away, and Day gently and gracefully made her appearance.

"It is so beautiful!" Rahab marvelled, as she watched the soft pearl-pink glow in the eastern sky, the shimmer of silver where the sunlight sparkled on the clear water of the stream, the glitter of gold as the sun's first rays touched the fields of wheat and barley far below.

Alone with her thoughts in the tranquility of early morning Rahab drew strength from the splendour of sunlight on the fields and streams, hills and valleys all around her. Deep within her she felt the warmth of hope burning in her heart, just as the sun's rays brought warmth and brightness to each new day. Since she had come to believe in Yahwey she had known a peace in her soul she had never thought possible. He who had created the magnificent panorama of earth and sky that lay before her, who had made the sun, the moon and the stars of heaven, could meet the deepest need of the human heart.

"He is the God of all gods," Rahab said with deep conviction, "and I believe in Him."

Rahab's house was conveniently situated on the high, deep outer walls of the city, and from her vantage point on the flat roof of her house she could see far and wide. Jericho was located in a beautiful, fertile oasis, and nature was lavish with her blessings. The broad plain, watered by the overflowing of the Jordan's banks once a year, yielded a bountiful harvest of fruit and crops, and the inhabitants of the small kingdom of Jericho never had to go hungry.

"Good morning Rahab. I see you are sky-watching as usual," said a voice teasingly.

Rahab turned around to greet her sister as she came up the stone steps.

"Yes, you know how I love it," she smiled. "But now that you are here we will get on with the day's work."

Her sister came each day to help Rahab with the daily chores, and one of their first tasks every morning was to arrange the long-stemmed stalks of flax on the flat roof of her house so that the warmth of the sun would dry them. When they were sufficiently cured they would make lamp wicks and ropes from the strong fibres which Rahab could sell as an added source of income to supplement the fees gained from her profession. For Rahab, her occupation was a living, and of necessity rather than choice.

Rahab and her sister talked as they worked. Their talk was usually about the happenings outside the city, tales which Rahab's clients brought each evening. In recent days the news was all about the Israelites who were encamped on the other side of the Jordan, and the thought of their impending invasion was already filling the citizens of Jericho with dread.

"Do you think they really will invade us?" asked Mirah worriedly.

"It seems likely," replied Rahab. "They attacked Sihon and Og and took their lands."

"But our city is well fortified with thick walls and stout gates," countered Mirah.

"Yes," agreed Rahab. "Our walls are immensely thick and strong."

"And our warriors are renowned for their might and valour," Mirah continued.

"Yes, they are," responded Rahab, "but I am sure the Israelite warriors are strong and skilled too, and in addition they have their God on their side."

"But they cannot cross the swollen Jordan river," reasoned Mirah. "The current is swift and the water is icy with the melting snows from Mount Hermon. They will have to wait till after the harvest at least, until the flooding in the valley subsides, and by that time we will have harvested our crops and stored the grain. We have our own water supply too, so we could withstand them for a long time."

"Maybe," said Rahab dubiously. "But have you not heard how their God rolled back the waters of the Red

Sea for them when they escaped from Egypt? All night long they travelled across the dry sea bed and reached the other side safely, but when Pharaoh's army followed them, this great God rolled the waters of the sea back again and the Egyptians were drowned."

"Yes, I have heard the story," admitted Mirah. "Rahab, I am afraid. I hope they will not come, but if they do, I hope they will not be able to enter our city."

Perhaps we can escape," said Rahab soothingly. "Let us not think any more about it just now. Look at that little silver stream weaving its way through the golden field of barley. Is it not beautiful?"

Her sister laughed.

"What a nature-lover you are!" she said as she ran down the steps. "You will come and see mother and father later?"

"Yes," promised Rahab.

The flax turning finished, Rahab gathered up the heavy length of rope she had plaited from the sturdy flax strands and curled it up in a corner. Then she sat on the low stone wall that was a safety feature of her flat-roofed house, and surveyed the scene around her.

To the west the mountains rose abruptly from the broad plain, while to the east, in the far distance the greeny-blue waters of the Jordan could just be glimpsed. The quiet, sun-washed landscape looked serene and peaceful, but in the light of what she had just been discussing with her sister, Rahab wondered how long it would remain so.

"The Israelites will come, sooner or later," she told herself. "Jericho can withstand them for a time, but they will win in the end."

Rahab found her thoughts turning again to Yahwey. She knew with certainty that He would help the Israelites. He was their God. But would he help her? Somehow, she felt she was under His protection.

"I believe He will," she said firmly, as if saying the words out loud would confirm them in her mind. "He is my God too."

The sun was rising higher in the sky now and there was much work to be done before the heat of the day sapped the strength and made toil seem burdensome. Although she and her girls practiced their profession in the hours after twilight, there was plenty to do during the day; wheat to be ground, bread to be baked, water to be carried, daily household duties to be performed.

She must visit her father and mother and see that they were well. They would speak together about Yahwey, the God of the Israelites, and she would encourage them again to trust in Him and not in gods of wood and stone who could neither hear nor help them. When she came back she would put on her rings and bracelets and sit for a while by her window where she could see and be seen.

Chapter 23

usk had fallen, and outside and in the deepening twilight the hurrying figures of the homeward-bound could barely be distinguished. In another few minutes as night-fall finally descended over the city, they would merge with the dusky shadows and become part of the night.

Rahab turned away from the window. It was time to light the lamps and prepare for the business of the evening.

"I wish I need not be part of it, " she murmured with a sigh, as she touched the long taper to an oil lamp fixed on the wall, and another in the centre of the room.

Behind her the door opened, and she swung around surprised. It was a little early for clients, but forcing a smile to her lips she turned to greet the men who had entered. They stood uncertainly in the doorway, tall dark shapes in the semi-darkness, but Rahab stepped forward quickly and drew them within the circle of the lamplight.

"Come in, you are welcome," she said brightly.

The instant she beheld them she could see that they were foreigners; their dress, their demeanour, their features, their obvious unease, indicated that they were not Canaanites. Rahab's heart lurched as some inner instinct told her who these men were. Before they had spoken even a word she knew with deep certainty that they were Israelites.

"May we obtain food and shelter here?" asked the taller of the two men somewhat hesitantly as he took in Rahab's dress and gaudy jewellery.

"That I can provide," replied Rahab with a smile. "Please sit down and I will bring food and wine."

She brought meat, bread and a platter of fruit and set it before them. She poured wine, and watched them as they ate and drank.

Unable to restrain herself any longer she asked, "May I enquire as to where you have come from?"

The men hesitated.

"From across the river," one replied evasively.

"I know that the Israelites are encamped beyond the river," ventured Rahab.

Without waiting for a reply she looked at them directly and said very quietly, "I believe you are Israelites."

The men looked startled and Rahab hastened to reassure them.

"Do not be afraid. I will not betray you. I will help you."

The men smiled their relief, the taller of the two letting his eyes rest on her with . . . was it admiration?

Rahab longed to talk to them about their God, but aware that others might enter her establishment at any minute she knew she must find a safe place for them.

"My girls will be here soon, and then we will have clients," she told them. "I must hide you before anyone sees you. Come with me."

She led the way to the stone stairwell, lifting a lamp of its sconce as she went. When they had climbed the steps and reached the flat roof of her house, Rahab heard the great gate in the walls of the city being closed and bolted so that none could enter or leave until morning.

"How did you know we are Israelites?" asked the tall man with interest.

"I just knew," replied Rahab with simple honesty. "I have been thinking about the Israelites for many weeks now."

"What do you know about us?" the tall man asked.

"I know what a powerful God you worship, and I want to know more about Him," Rahab said eagerly.

"What would you like to know?" he asked, again looking at her with a strangely gentle expression in his eyes.

"I want to know why God helps the Israelites so much."

"Because He chose us to be His people and He loves us," he replied.

"Will He help anyone who trusts in Him?" asked Rahab.

"Yes," said the tall Israelite confidently.

Downstairs the door clanged and Rahab heard the voices of her companions. She knew she must go. The girls would wonder where she was and might come looking for her. It was vital to keep the Israelites concealed.

"Quickly," she told the men urgently. "Lie down and I will cover you with the stalks of flax. You will be safe here. I will come back as soon as I can. We will talk then."

Running hastily down the steps she returned to the room below which the girls had just entered. She stood in the shadows for a moment to catch her breath and calm herself. Her encounter with the Israelites had unnerved her, and she needed a little time to collect her thoughts. She felt the burden of responsibility for their safety lying heavily upon her, and she was well aware of the danger to herself if they were found in her house.

"I am certain they are safely hidden," she told herself, but she was nervous.

As she moved into the room and greeted her companions two or three men entered, and soon they were all talking and laughing together. The distraction took Rahab's mind off her immediate anxiety. She suggested some music and dancing but before the girls could start there was a loud banging at the door, and it was suddenly flung open to reveal several men of the king's guard who entered unceremoniously and immediately addressed Rahab.

"The king has sent us to tell you to bring out the men who came to you and entered your house, because they have come to spy out the whole land."

There was a gasp from one of the girls and suddenly all eyes were on Rahab. She felt her mouth go dry, but she forced herself to remain calm.

"Yes, the men came to me," she admitted, "but I did not know where they had come from. At dusk, when it was time to close the city gate, the men left. I do not know which way they went. Go after them quickly. You may catch up with them."

The guards seemed satisfied and left as quickly as they had come.

For a moment there was a stunned silence, then everyone began talking at once.

"Were they Israelites? What were they like?"

"What did they ask you?"

"They came to spy on us."

"What did you tell them?"

"I am afraid. What will become of us?"

Rahab held up her hand to stop the barrage of questions. Her legs were shaking and her heart was pounding.

"They asked me nothing, and I told them nothing," she said as firmly as she could. "They wanted food, I gave them food and then they left. That's all I can tell you."

The door opened again and one or two more men entered. Rahab bustled about pouring wine for them, while the others were quick to tell them the news, and before long they were all engrossed in discussing this latest information.

"Let us have some music and dancing," suggested Rahab, trying to deflect the conversation away from the Israelites.

But the men wanted to talk about nothing else, and the girls did not feel like dancing. The sobering event of the evening had dampened the spirits of both men and girls, and as Rahab listened to their conversation she realised afresh just how much fear there was in the city. With the mood so sombre the activities of the evening ended earlier than usual and everyone went home.

As soon as she was alone, Rahab sped upstairs again to speak to the Israelites.

"I know that the Lord has given this land to you and that a great fear of you has fallen on us, so that all who live in this country are melting in fear because of you," she began.

The men looked at each other in surprise.

Rahab continued, "We have heard how the Lord dried up the water of the Red Sea for you when you came out of Egypt, and what you did to Sihon and Og, the two kings of the Amorites east of the Jordan, whom you completely destroyed. When we heard of it, our hearts sank and everyone's courage failed because of you, for the Lord your God is God in heaven above and on the earth below."

Again the Israelites looked surprised and pleased as they listened to Rahab.

Earnestly Rahab continued, " Now, please swear to me by the Lord that you will show kindness to my family, because I have shown kindness to you. Give me a sure sign that you will spare the lives of my father and mother, my brothers and sisters, and all who belong to them, and that you will save us from death."

"Our lives for your lives!" the tall Israelite assured her sincerely. "If you do not tell what we are doing, we will treat you kindly and faithfully when the Lord gives us the land."

Rahab smiled with relief and gratitude, but she knew she must help them escape though she was loath to let them go.

"You have been seen," she told them, "and the king knows you are in Jericho, but I have told his messengers that you have gone, and they have already left in pursuit of you. Now you must go to the hills so that the pursuers will not find you. Hide yourselves there three days until they return, and then go on your way."

She lifted the heavy rope which she had placed in the corner of the roof earlier in the day. It was strong enough to take their weight as they descended down the wall.

The tall Israelite took her hands in his and spoke gently.

"This oath you made us swear will not be binding on us unless, when we enter the land, you have tied this scarlet cord in the window through which you let us down, and unless you have brought your father and mother, your brothers and all your family into your house."

Rahab nodded and the other Israelite continued.

"If anyone goes outside your house into the street, his blood will be on his own head; we will not be responsible. As for anyone who is in the house with you, his blood will be on our head if a hand is laid on him."

Again Rahab nodded.

"But if you tell what we are doing, we will be released from the oath you have made us swear," he warned.

"I agree," promised Rahab. "Let it be as you say."

The tall young Israelite took the long heavy rope from Rahab's hands and tied it firmly in place. He turned to her again and spoke gently.

"May I ask your name?" he enquired.

Rahab felt her heart beating a little faster as she looked up at him.

"My name is Rahab," she smiled. "Will you tell me yours?"

"Salmon," he said, looking at her steadily. "I hope to see you again soon Rahab."

Rahab took the rope into her hands as the men prepared to slide down. With a last smile and a wave they were gone. She drew the rope up again in case it should be seen by anyone at daylight, but she would place it in position once more before the Israelites came into the country.

As she went slowly downstairs she could not help thinking of the tall young Israelite who had spoken to her so kindly. Was he really looking forward to seeing her again?

"I would like to see him again, but why would he want a girl like me?" she sighed.

Still, it was a pleasant thought that they would meet again, and a comforting thought to know that the men had given their word that she and her family would be safe.

"I will dream about Salmon tonight," she smiled to herself as she lay down for the night.

Chapter 24

The city was in turmoil. Fear and consternation lived in every heart since news had come that the entire nation of Israel had crossed the River Jordan and were encamped at Gilgal on the city's eastern border. Their army was at the ready, armed and prepared for battle on the plains of Jericho.

"Rahab, what are we going to do?" cried Mirah, almost hysterical.

"We will gather all the family together in my house," Rahab said calmly. "Do not be afraid."

She ran up the stone steps to the roof and hastily let down the red rope over the wall. With the gates of the city securely bolted and no-one entering or leaving, it would be seen only by the Israelites when they reached the walls of the city.

"Let us bring father and mother and the whole family here now," she said. "Then we will all be safe."

"Are you sure we will be safe?" asked Mirah anxiously.

"Yes, I am sure," responded Rahab with quiet confidence.

She trusted implicitly in the assurance she had been given by the Israelite spies. She and all belonging to her would be saved. She trusted too in their God.

"Let us trust in the God of the Israelites," she told Mirah. "He is a powerful God."

The story of how the Israelites had crossed the river was spreading quickly all over the city. An eye witness described how the waters from both upstream and downstream stopped flowing and stood up in a heap. Miraculously a dry path was created in the river so that the people could cross, and it remained dry until they had all reached the other side, then the waters returned to their place and flowed naturally.

"What do you think of a God like that!" said Rahab excitedly. "Is He not amazing?"

Rahab was glad her family members were beginning to understand more about the Almighty God the

Israelites worshipped. This latest miraculous event, so like the Red Sea story, demonstrated the power of God, and her mother and father, brothers and sisters could see that He was able to do mighty acts which their false Canaanite gods were powerless to perform.

"Trust in this God!" urged Rahab. "He is the one true God."

As they waited in the safety of Rahab's house, outside the city walls the Israelite army had begun to march around the city. Nervously the citizens of Jericho watched as the Israelites marched confidently day after day.

For six days they marched once around the walls, but on the seventh day they continued to march until they had completed seven circuits. Rahab and her family observed them from the window of her house on the walls, secure in the knowledge that the red rope was in position, and would be their salvation.

"It will be all right," Rahab told her family reassuringly. "The men promised that we would all be saved. Our lives for theirs, they said."

Suddenly there was a deafening shout which seemed to reverberate around the whole city, and to their dismay the walls began to crumble. They heard the great city gates fall with a mighty crash, and the Israelite army rush in.

"Rahab!" called a voice that she knew.

He was there, tall, handsome and smiling.

"Rahab, it is wonderful to see you again!"

"I am glad to see you too," Rahab said shyly.

For a moment they gazed at each other, oblivious to all around them. Then Salmon moved swiftly into action.

"Come," he said. "Bring your family and follow me. I will take you to safety."

They followed the young Israelite as he led them outside the city, away from the noise and confusion, to a quiet place just beyond the camp of the Israelites. Tents had been erected for them, and servants were preparing food for them.

"We are so grateful, Salmon," said Rahab.

"We gave you our promise," he responded, "and we have fulfilled it."

"I knew you would," smiled Rahab. "I trusted you."

"And I wanted to see you again," he said looking deeply into her eyes.

Rahab felt her heart racing.

"Rahab," he said softly. "I am falling in love with you."

She raised her eyes to his and gazed at him wonderingly.

"I want to marry you Rahab," he continued with deep sincerity.

She was hearing words she never thought to hear.

"You would marry a girl like me?" she questioned.

He nodded.

"Because I love you, because you believe in my God, and because you did not betray us to the king of Jericho." he said. "You are a wonderful girl Rahab."

Tears of happiness filled Rahab's eyes. Love! This was what she had been waiting for all her life. She had never imagined that she would be loved by such a man as Salmon; a devoted worshipper of Yahwey, a man of courage and integrity, a man who offered her the dignity of marriage. She had never known such a man.

She looked up at him, her eyes shining with happiness.

"I love you too," she said.

Chapter 25

The journey to Bethlehem would be long and beset with sadness. As the three women trudged along the road together, each was acutely aware of their plight. Poor and widowed, with no means of support, they were sorrowful and downcast in spirit.

"Naomi especially," thought Ruth. "And no wonder! She has lost all who were dear to her, both her sons and her husband."

She knew her mother-in-law was heartbroken, but she had determined that she would return to her own land, and Ruth hoped it would bring her some comfort to be among her own people again.

They had left Moab at first light, and had travelled until they were weary and thirsty, so they stopped to rest and have a drink from their water skins. Naomi looked at her daughters-in law, and it hurt Ruth to see the grief and anguish in her eyes.

"Go back, each of you, to your mother's house. May the Lord show kindness to you, as you have shown to your dead and to me. May the Lord grant that each of you will find rest in the home of another husband."

As Naomi put her arms around her to kiss her goodbye, Ruth burst into tears. Beside her Orpah too was sobbing. Naomi seemed so vulnerable, so fragile, so alone. How could they think of leaving her?

"We will go back with you to your people," they said together.

But Naomi shook her head, tears flowing down her cheeks.

"Return home, my daughters. Why would you come with me? Am I going to have any more sons, who could become your husbands? Return home, my daughters. I am too old to have another husband. Even if I thought there was still hope for me—even if I had a husband tonight and then gave birth to sons—would you wait until they grew up? Would you remain unmarried for them? No, my daughters; for it grieves me very much for your sakes that the hand of the Lord has gone out against me."

The girls wept afresh at these words as they stood in each other's embrace. Then finally Orpah kissed her mother-in-law goodbye and returned on her way to Moab, but Ruth clung to her.

Naomi turned to her. "Look," she said, "your sister-in-law is going back to her people and her gods. Go back with her."

Ruth clasped her arms more tightly around her mother-in-law, and knew with complete certainty that she could not leave her. She loved this little woman who had suffered such adversity, and she would stay with her no matter what the consequences might be or where it would lead her.

"Entreat me not to leave you, or to turn back from following after you; For wherever you go, I will go; And wherever you lodge, I will lodge; Your people shall be my people, and your God, my God. Where you die, I will die, and there will I be buried. The Lord do so to me, and more also, if anything but death parts you and me."

Naomi's face was wet with tears, but brushing them away she smiled lovingly at her daughter-in-law. Ruth held her close for another moment, then they went on together.

It took many days of weary travelling to reach Bethlehem, but at last they came to the little town in the hill country of Judah just as the barley harvest was beginning.

They created quite a stir in the small community as they arrived in the town. Although Naomi had left ten years previously, Ruth could see that many of the women remembered her with fondness.

"Can this be Naomi?" they exclaimed as they gathered around her.

Clearly she was much changed. Sorrow had etched lines of pain on her face and her eyes were sad and forlorn.

"Do not call me Naomi," she told them. "Call me Mara, because the Almighty has dealt very bitterly with me. I went out full, and the Lord has brought me back empty. Why call me Naomi? The Lord has afflicted me; the Almighty has brought misfortune upon me."

Naomi poured out the whole tragic story of how her husband Elimelech had died, and then after a period of time her two sons, who had married Moabite girls, had also died. The women sympathised deeply with her, and then accompanied her, along with Ruth, to the piece of land that had belonged to Elimelech and the little house that was still there.

It was a sad homecoming for Naomi, Ruth reflected, but at least she was back where she belonged. Perhaps she could better recover from her sorrow among her own people where she had the comfort of friends around her.

Chapter 26

The following morning Ruth arose early. With the barley harvest just started she knew there was something she could do to provide food for Naomi and herself.

"Let me go to the fields and pick up the leftover grain behind anyone in whose eyes I find favour," she said to Naomi.

"Go my daughter," replied her mother-in-law.

Ruth had learned that it was customary in Israel for widows and foreigners to be permitted to glean in the fields after the harvesters. It was a law in the land that they must look after the poor who could not look after themselves. No-one should be allowed to starve.

As she worked diligently to pick up the stray stalks of barley left behind by the harvesters, the owner of the field arrived, and Ruth discovered that his name was Boaz.

"The Lord be with you," he greeted the harvesters.

They called back, "The Lord bless you."

Ruth could see that Boaz had noticed her, and when she saw him speaking to his servant who was in charge of the harvesting, she deduced that he was probably enquiring about her. This was confirmed when he came over to her.

"My daughter, listen to me," he said kindly. "Do not go and glean in another field and do not go away from here. Stay here with my servant girls. Watch the field where the men are harvesting, and follow along after the girls. I have commanded the young men not to touch you. And whenever you are thirsty, go and get a drink from the water jars the men have filled."

Ruth was amazed and touched by his consideration of her, a foreigner and a stranger, and she bowed low out of respect for him.

"Why have I found such favour in your eyes that you notice me—a foreigner?" she exclaimed.

Boaz replied, "I have been told all about what you have done for your mother-in-law since the death of your husband—how you left your father and mother and your homeland and came to live with a people you did not know before. May the Lord repay you for what you have done. May you be richly rewarded by the Lord, the God of Israel, under whose wings you have come to take refuge."

"May I continue to find favour in your eyes, my lord," Ruth replied. "You have given me comfort and have spoken kindly to your servant—though I do not have the standing of one of your servant girls."

Boaz's warm words moved Ruth deeply. She could see that he was a kind and caring man who took to heart the welfare of poor people like herself and Naomi.

She worked on in the sunshine, enjoying the fragrance of the freshly-cut barley, and the sense of wellbeing she felt from the kindness of Boaz, and from being able to glean in his field, unhindered and unafraid.

When mealtime came Boaz called to her.

"Come over here. Have some bread and dip it in the wine vinegar."

As soon as she sat down with the harvesters Boaz offered her some roasted grain. Ruth, who had endured hunger oftentimes on the journey to Bethlehem, enjoyed the wholesome food with a feeling of deep satisfaction and gratitude. When she had eaten enough of the grain to satisfy her, she kept some of it back to take home to Naomi.

As she got up again to return to her gleaning she heard Boaz giving orders to his men concerning her.

"Let her glean even among the sheaves, and do not reproach her. Also let grain from the bundles fall purposely for her; leave it so that she may glean, and do not rebuke her."

"How generous and thoughtful he is!" she marvelled to herself.

When the evening came, Ruth threshed the barley she had picked and then trudged back to the town, tired, but overwhelmed at the success of her day's work which had been brought about by the benevolence of Boaz.

"Where did you glean today?" asked Naomi as she caught sight of the plentiful heap of barley Ruth placed in front of her. "Blessed be the man who took notice of you."

"The name of the man I worked with today is Boaz," she told her.

Animatedly, she described how generous and caring he had been towards her.

"The Lord bless him," exclaimed Naomi. "He has not stopped showing his kindness to the living and the dead. That man is our close relative; he is one of our kinsman-redeemers."

Ruth could see that Naomi was cheered by the kindness and generosity of Boaz, and it gladdened her heart. And it was good to know he was a relative. Perhaps it explained why he had been so magnanimous. He had a duty towards them.

"He even said to me, 'Stay with my workers until they have finished harvesting all my grain,'" Ruth said happily.

"It will be good for you, my daughter, to go with his girls, because in someone else's field you might be harmed," Naomi told her.

So each morning Ruth set off for the fields of Boaz, and returned each evening with her bundle of grain which was enough to feed her mother-in-law and herself for some time to come. As she observed the courteous and kindly behaviour of Boaz, not only towards herself, but his servants as well, her esteem for him grew daily, and she knew that she was witnessing a truly godly man who was an example of all that was best in the Hebrew religion. Their God, in whom she had come to trust, had taught them to care for the poor and needy, the widows and foreigners, and Boaz was fulfilling the precepts of his God to perfection.

Ruth found herself thinking of him often.

"What a good man he is!" she said, smiling to herself as she reflected on his kind attention to her. "The Lord has been so good to me."

Chapter 27

"My daughter, shall I not seek security for you, that it may be well with you?" said Naomi one day. "Now Boaz, whose young women you were with, is he not our relative?"

At the mention of his name Ruth found herself blushing. She admitted that she admired Boaz, and she perceived that her mother-in-law had discerned that Boaz was attracted to her because of the attention he had shown her.

"Therefore," continued Naomi, "wash yourself and perfume yourself, put on your best garment and go down to the threshing floor; but do not make yourself known to him until he has finished eating and drinking. Then when he lies down, notice the place where he lies; then go and uncover his feet and lie down. He will tell you what you should do."

"All that you say to me I will do," Ruth replied.

So that evening, dressed in her best garments, she went down to the threshing floor where Boaz was winnowing his barley. Since he was the owner, it fell to him to protect his own property so he was alone. Ruth stayed out of sight until he had finished eating and drinking and had fallen asleep in a corner of the threshing floor, then she crept over to him, uncovered his feet, and lay down.

In the middle of the night Ruth stirred and realised that Boaz had awakened and had become aware of someone lying there.

"Who are you?" he asked.

"I am your servant Ruth," she said, her voice tremulous. "Spread the corner of your garment over me, since you are a kinsman-redeemer."

"Blessed are you of the Lord, my daughter!" replied Boaz. "For you have shown more kindness at the end than at the beginning, in that you did not go after young men, whether poor or rich. And now, my daughter, do not fear. I will do for you all that you request, for all the people of my town know that you are a virtuous woman."

Relief flooded over Ruth at his gracious words. So he did care for her!

"Now it is true that I am a close relative," continued Boaz. "However there is a relative closer than I. Stay this night, and in the morning it shall be that if he will perform the duty of a close relative for you—good: let him do it. But if he does not want to perform the duty for you, then I will perform the duty for you, as the Lord lives! Lie down until morning."

As she lay down again Ruth's thoughts were in turmoil. There was a nearer kinsman-redeemer! What if he redeemed Naomi's land and not Boaz! The thought dismayed her, for Boaz had spoken warmly, even tenderly to her, and she so hoped that he would be the one to play the part of the kinsman-redeemer. She knew it meant more than merely buying the land. It would mean marriage, which was what Naomi intended for her, and what she would wish for herself.

Before dawn Ruth stirred once more and got up to go. Boaz too awoke.

"Do not let it be known that a woman came to the threshing floor," he said.

As she prepared to leave Boaz stopped her.

"Bring me the shawl you are wearing and hold it out," he said.

He poured six measures of barley into it, and helped her to put it on her back.

As soon as she returned home Naomi asked, "How did it go, my daughter?"

Ruth related everything that Boaz had said, and as she listened Naomi nodded knowingly.

"He gave me these six measures of barley," Ruth finished, "and he said 'Do not go home to your mother-in-law empty-handed.'"

"Wait, my daughter, until you find out what happens," Naomi said sagely, "For the man will not rest until the matter is settled today."

Naomi was right. Boaz came to them later in the morning. He had settled the matter. The elders at the town gate had acknowledged him as their kinsman-redeemer, and had pronounced their blessing.

"We are witnesses. May the Lord make the woman who is coming into your home like Rachel and Leah, who together built up the house of Israel. May you have standing in Ephrathah and be famous in Bethlehem. Through the offspring the Lord gives you by this young woman, may your family be like that of Perez, whom Tamar bore to Judah."

Ruth smiled happily as Boaz looked at her with eyes full of love.

The day of their wedding was a joyful occasion, and the following year when her son was born, Ruth placed him lovingly in Naomi's lap.

"Praise be to the Lord, who this day has not left you without a kinsman-redeemer," the women said. "May he become famous throughout Israel! He will renew your life and sustain you in old age. For your daughter-in-law, who loves you and who is better to you than seven sons, has given him birth."

Ruth was overjoyed to see happiness return again to her mother-in-law. She had known such sorrow, but now there was joy. With Boaz and herself, and now little Obed to keep her company she need never be lonely again.

"Naomi has a son," the women said.

The years of hardship melted away. She and Naomi could rest content now, knowing that the Lord had not forsaken them, but had blessed them abundantly, and had given them a rich heritage in the land of Judah.

Chapter 28

*I*t was spring time in Jerusalem. Sun warmed the cobbled streets and flat roofs of the houses, the blossoms on the almond trees were flourishing profusely, and birds sang gladly in the branches.

The city was quiet in the spring sunshine. King David had sent his army out to battle under the command of Joab, his chief, although he himself remained in his palace.

"This must be the first time the king has not gone out with his men," observed Bathsheba. "He is such a mighty warrior it is strange he has stayed at home."

King David's prowess as a warrior was well-known. He had achieved many successful campaigns against the Philistines, and numerous triumphs in other battles, and he was highly regarded among the people. He was popular, not just for his fighting ability, but for his godly character and generosity of spirit. In addition he was gifted in music and poetry, and was a man of great charm and charisma.

"A man among men!" mused Bathsheba.

Although she had never met him she had seen him often and admired him greatly.

She strolled around the courtyard of her home, her thoughts engaged with the king, the army and in particular her husband. She had not been married long to Uriah, who was one of the king's elite force of mighty men, a considerable warrior in his own right.

Often she had wondered why her father, who was also one of the king's mighty men, had married her to this man. He was a Hittite, and according to the Laws God gave to Moses, the Israelites were forbidden to marry Hittites. Still, Uriah was a man of noble character, not unlike the king, brave, honourable and loyal. She liked and respected him, but she was not in love with him. Perhaps that would come later.

"I wish . . ." began Bathsheba. "No, I must not think this way."

But the thought persisted.

"I wish," she said to herself, "that I could have married a man from my own tribe of Judah. It would have been more . . fitting. After all, my name is Bathsheba, daughter of the promise."

Bathsheba reflected on that important promise which God had given away back in the Garden of Eden. Although spoken to the serpent, it had given hope to Eve.

Since the days of their ancestors every woman in the tribe of Judah aspired to be the one to give birth to the son who would eventually destroy the power of the Evil One, and deliver mankind from the curse of sin.

"If Uriah and I have a son he will not belong to the clan of Judah," Bathsheba contemplated with a sigh.

She grew wistful and a little petulant at the thought.

"Since I am daughter of the promise it would have been wonderful to have given birth to the son of the promise."

She sighed as she continued to wander around the courtyard. Stopping by the little pool she gazed into the clear water. The late afternoon air was balmy, and the pool looked inviting.

"Why not?" she smiled.

There was no-one in the soldiers' quarters, the men having all gone out to battle, including her husband, so it was safe to bathe. No one would see her.

She slipped off her outer robe and her sandals, stepped into the pool and splashed the cool water around her face and arms. The water refreshed and revived her and she began to feel more energised. After a while, when she had finished washing, she sat on the edge of the pool and let the sun dry her skin.

Bathsheba sat silently for a time, enjoying the pleasant warmth of the sun on her body, then stirred as one of her maidservants appeared before her.

"Messengers have come from King David," the maid told her. "They wish to speak with you."

Hastily Bathsheba drew her robe about her and slipped her feet into her sandals.

"The king requests your company," the messengers told her. "We are here to escort you to him."

Surprised, Bathsheba stared at them wide-eyed for a moment. It was an honour to be invited into the king's presence, but why would he ask for her? He did not know her.

The men were waiting. She supposed she could not refuse.

"As the king wishes," she said simply.

Bathsheba's heart was pounding as she bowed low before the king, but he took her hands and gently drew her upwards. He was smiling as he looked deeply into her eyes, and she caught her breath.

How handsome he was, and how charming!

"You are so beautiful Bathsheba," he murmured. "When I saw you in your courtyard earlier, I longed to meet you."

Bathsheba started and blushed.

"You . . . you saw me?" she stammered.

"Forgive me," he apologised, kissing the back of her hand.

He smiled his charming smile and her heart melted. She could not help smiling back at him.

"I was walking on my roof-top," he explained coyly, "and I happened to see the most beautiful woman I have ever seen."

He smiled down at her once again, and then he took her hand.

"Come and see," he said.

He led her on to his flat roof and pointed to her court-yard which she could see was not far away. Of necessity his chief warriors were housed close to the Palace.

David drew her inside again, and took her face in his hands.

"I just had to meet you Bathsheba," he said softly. "You are exquisitely beautiful."

Next moment his lips were on hers and his kiss was ecstasy!. He swept her into his arms and held her close. Guilt and delight alternatively gripped Bathsheba. She must not, she should not do this, but could she resist the king, and did she want to?

Time stood still, two hearts beat with passion, and Bathsheba, finally surrendering the last vestige of her resistance, yielded to the embrace of David, king of Israel.

Chapter 29

"Adultery!" whispered Bathsheba. "I committed adultery!"

She could not even bring herself to say the word aloud. She paced up and down in anguish of soul. She had transgressed the law which God had given through Moses. Adultery was forbidden, and the consequences for breaking it were grave.

"I knew it was wrong, but I could not help myself," she groaned.

But it had been King David who had sent for her, and it was he who had seduced her. Could she have refused the king? Perhaps, but she acknowledged to herself that she had not tried to stop him.

"Not only do I feel great guilt, but I am with child," she cried, " and I do not know what to do."

Bathsheba wept afresh and flung herself on her bed in deep distress. There was no-one she could confide in, no-one she could tell. . . except . . .

"Of course!" she breathed, suddenly sitting upright. "The king must be told. I will send him word immediately. If he is the honourable man I believe him to be he will take responsibility for his actions, and tell me what to do."

She wrote her letter to the king and sent it by the hand of her most trusted maidservant. Now she would have to wait and see what would happen.

Snippets of information filtered through to her. She heard that Uriah was back in Jerusalem, but he had not come home, choosing instead to sleep in the guardroom at the Palace. Then news came that he had returned to the battlefield.

Finally word was brought to her that he had been killed in battle. Bathsheba was shocked and grieved. He had been a good man, a noble man, and she had betrayed his trust. For that she felt deep regret.

"My only comfort is that he did not know of my unfaithfulness," she thought.

A month was the traditional period of mourning for the loss of a loved one. It allowed Bathsheba time to grieve and come to terms with all that had happened. She had not loved Uriah but she regretted his death. Infidelity had never crossed her mind until king David had sent for her. She was full of contrition and had repented before her God. She wondered if David had done the same.

When the period of mourning was completed King David sent for her and she became his wife. She could rest now before the birth of her baby.

"Strange!" she said to herself. "I wished for a child from the clan of Judah. Now my child will be a son of David who is the head of Judah."

The thought gave her pleasure, though her heart was still sad over the events surrounding it. She knew by this time that King David had sent Uriah into the thick of the battle knowing that he would almost certainly be slain.

When her baby was born Bathsheba forgot all the sorrow of the past months and thought only of the joy of his birth. David too was delighted with his small son.

Bathsheba was so rapturously happy with her baby that she did not at first notice that he was becoming ill.

"What is wrong with my baby?" she asked panic-stricken.

As the days passed he became worse. David had taken to fasting and praying for the child. He refused to eat, and lay all night on the ground before the Lord.

Bathsheba had been so occupied with her baby that she had taken no notice when Nathan the prophet came to see David. Now she guessed that Nathan had brought word from the Lord concerning the child.

When the baby was seven days old he died. Bathsheba was heart-broken. Her sweet little baby, the child of clan Judah she had so longed for. She was desolate.

David came to her in the evening after he had washed, put on fresh clothes and worshipped in the house of the Lord. His eyes were sad as he gazed into hers.

"My servants asked why I requested food now that our baby has gone, when I fasted while he was still alive" he began.

"What did you tell them?"asked Bathsheba dully.

"I said, 'While the child was still alive, I fasted and wept. I thought, "Who knows? The Lord may be gracious to me and let the child live." But now that he is dead, why should I fast? Can I bring him back again? I will go to him, but he will not return to me'."

At this Bathsheba laid her head on his shoulder and wept sorely. David held her tenderly and comforted her.

"Nathan the prophet came to me with word from the Lord God of Israel," David told her. "I confessed to him that I had sinned against the Lord, and he told me the child would not live."

Bathsheba nodded. There was nothing more to be said.

After a time, David expressed his contrition in a beautiful poem which was a prayer from the depths of his soul. It brought tears to Bathsheba's eyes when she heard it.

"Have mercy upon me, O God, according to your unfailing love;

According to your great compassion blot out my transgressions;

Wash away all my iniquity and cleanse me from my sin.

For I know my transgressions, and my sin is always before me.

Against You, You only, I have sinned and done what is evil in Your sight,

So that You are proved right when You speak and justified when you judge.

Save me from bloodguilt, O God, the God who saves me,

And my tongue will sing of your righteousness."

Later, knowing God's forgiveness, David composed other beautiful verses.

"He does not treat us as our sins deserve or repay us according to our iniquities,

For as high as the heavens are above the earth,

So great is His love for those who fear Him;

As far as the east is from the west,

So far has he removed our transgressions from us."

"God has been so good to us," Bathsheba declared fervently.

He had shown His love, mercy and forgiveness. Since the death of their firstborn, four more sons had been born to them; Solomon, Nathan, Shammua and Shobab.

"I am blessed," Bathsheba said humbly. "Daughter of the promise, I have had a part to play in the clan of Judah."

Chapter 30

athsheba was sitting sadly contemplating the condition of her husband David. He was old; long years of hardship and war had taken their toll, and his health was rapidly declining. Once so active, he was now confined to bed.

She stirred when Nathan the prophet arrived to speak with her. Nathan had been such a friend to the king and herself through the years, and they had named their second son after him.

Nathan spoke urgently.

"Have you not heard that Adonijah, the son of Haggith, has become king without our lord David's knowing it? Now then, let me advise you how you can save your own life and the life of your son Solomon."

Bathsheba was greatly alarmed by what she was hearing.

Nathan continued, "Go immediately to King David and say to him, 'My lord the king, did you not swear to me your maidservant saying, "Assuredly your son Solomon shall reign after me, and he shall sit on my throne"? Why then has Adonijah become king?'"

It was true. David had promised that her son Solomon would be king after him. It was because the Lord had shown His favour towards Solomon and He had chosen him.

"While you are still there talking with the king," finished Nathan, "I will come in and confirm what you have said."

Bathsheba hastened to the king.

"What is your wish?" David asked.

Since it was a formal request relating to the kingdom, and not a personal visit, Bathsheba bowed low before the king.

"My lord, you yourself swore to me your servant by the Lord your God: 'Solomon your son shall become king after me, and he will sit on my throne.' But now Adonijah has become king, and you, my lord the king, do not know about it."

She proceeded to tell him all that Adonijah had done to set himself up as king.

"My lord the king," she finished, "the eyes of all Israel are on you, that you should tell them who will sit on the throne of my lord the king after him. Otherwise, it will happen, when my lord the king rests with his fathers, that I and my son Solomon will be counted as offenders."

Before she had finished speaking Nathan the prophet arrived and he was granted entry to the king's presence.

Nathan spoke at once. "Have you, my lord the king, declared that Adonijah shall be king after you, and that he will sit on your throne?"

Nathan reinforced everything that Bathsheba had already told the king, and finished by saying, "Is this something my lord the king has done without letting his servants know who should sit on the throne of my lord the king after him?"

This stirred the king to action.

"Call Bathsheba to me," he said at once.

"As surely as the Lord lives, who has delivered me from every distress," David told her, "I will surely carry out today what I swore to you by the Lord, the God of

Israel: Solomon your son shall be king after me, and he will sit on my throne in my place."

Bathsheba bowed low before the king and said, with great relief and gratitude, "May my lord King David live forever!"

Then King David said, "Call in Zadoz the priest, Nathan the prophet and Benaiah."

When they entered the king's presence Bathsheba listened gladly while David gave instructions for the anointing of Solomon as king of Israel.

"Take your lord's servants with you and set Solomon my son on my own mule and take him down to Gihon. There shall Zadok the priest and Nathan the prophet anoint him king over Israel. Blow the trumpet and shout, 'Long live King Solomon!' Then you are to go up with him, and he is to come and sit on my throne and reign in my place. I have appointed him ruler over Israel and Judah."

It was done with speed, but it was performed in accordance with perfect protocol. Zadok the priest took a horn of oil from the tabernacle and anointed Solomon. The trumpet was blown and all the people shouted, "Long live King Solomon!" There was music and great joy, and all the people rejoiced heartily with singing, shouting and much excitement and happiness.

Bathsheba heard later that Adonijah gave up without a fight since his friends took fear and deserted him.

King David himself, relieved and happy that Solomon's anointing had taken place said, "Blessed be the Lord God of Israel who has allowed my eyes to see a successor on my throne today."

As Bathsheba knelt by her window at the day's end, it was with deep thankfulness. Her son Solomon was king. God had accomplished His purpose through Nathan the prophet, King David and herself. David's throne was established as God had promised.

Years before Nathan had been sent to bring David a prophecy from the Lord.

"Your house and your kingdom shall endure for ever before Me; your throne shall be established for ever." God had said.

At that time David was so touched by God's amazing promise that he sat in great humility before the Lord and prayed.

"Who am I, O Sovereign Lord, and what is my family, that you have brought me this far? . . . How great You are, O Sovereign Lord! There is no-one like You. . . . You have established Your people Israel as your very own for ever, and You, O Lord, have become their God."

At the end of his prayer David worshipped the Lord.

"O Sovereign Lord, You are God! Your words are trustworthy, and you have promised these good things to your servant. Now be pleased to bless the house of Your servant that it may continue for ever in your sight; for You, O Sovereign Lord, have spoken, and with Your blessing the house of Your servant will be blessed for ever."

Bathsheba bowed in reverent praise at the memory of these words. Today God had begun the fulfilment of His promise in the anointing of Solomon, and she knew He would continue to perpetuate the House of David, of the line of Judah.

She thought back to David's ancestry in the clan of Judah.

"Sarah was told kings would come from her; Jacob,her grandson, later to be known as Israel, proph-esied that the sceptre would never depart from Judah, her great–grandson."

Bathsheba's thoughts drifted to the women who, though not Israelites, had become believers in the God of Israel, had married Israelite men, and had sons with them.

"Tamar gave Judah Perez, Rahab and Salmon had Boaz. Ruth married Boaz and their son Obed was the father of Jesse who was the father of David, and David was the first bearer of the sceptre!"

The more she thought about it the more excited Bathsheba became.

"Now my son Solomon bears the sceptre!" she said proudly.

Then she suddenly felt humble. In spite of the shameful beginning of her relationship with David, God had forgiven and blessed them abundantly. Her four sons were all good young men, but King David had married other wives before he met her, and sadly some of his other sons had shown a rebellious nature.

"Solomon is a godly young man," she said thankfully, "and Nathan too. I trust he will take after our faithful friend and prophet for whom he is named. I believe all my sons are good men."

Bathsheba felt deeply thankful.

"I am daughter of the promise," she smiled, "and my sons are the sons of the king of Judah. It was meant to be."

Chapter 31

The little town of Nazareth lay in a valley amidst the southernmost hills of Lebanon in the region of Galilee. It was a strange place to find families from the clan of Judah, but some had wandered from the Judean hills to settle in this peaceful and pretty little town, which had the advantage of being close to a major trade route.

Mary's family was just such a family. Although directly descended from King David, they were reduced to more humble circumstances, like many of the people of Israel after the Exile, and they had settled here in the hope of making a modest living.

Evening quiet had descended upon the town. Work had ended for the day, and the townsfolk were resting from their labours. Mary too had finished her daily duties and was sitting in pensive mood in a secluded spot on a hillside near her home, when she suddenly became aware of a glorious brightness all around her. Looking up, her gaze fell upon a shining angelic being who immediately addressed her in a most surprising manner.

"Greetings, you who are highly favoured! The Lord is with you."

Mary was troubled by these words. She could not imagine what they meant or why they were spoken to her.

"Do not be afraid Mary," the angel continued. "You have found favour with God. You will be with child and give birth to a son, and you are to give him the name Jesus. He will be great and will be called the Son of the Most High. The Lord will give him the throne of his father David, and he will reign over the house of Jacob for ever."

Astonishing words! Mary was overwhelmed by them as her mind struggled to comprehend them. There was one question she needed to ask.

"How will this be, since I am a virgin?"

The answer was equally astounding.

"The Holy Spirit will come upon you, and the power of the Most High will overshadow you. So the Holy One to be born of you will be called the Son of God."

Mary caught her breath. The Son of God!

The angel had more to say, and Mary listened in wonder.

"Even Elizabeth your relative is going to have a child in her old age, and she who was said to be barren is in her sixth month. For nothing is impossible with God."

"I am the Lord's servant," Mary answered humbly. "May it be to me as you have said."

The angel departed, leaving her awed and filled with a strange joy.

She turned the words the angel had spoken over and over in her mind: "You have found favour with God . . . you will give birth to a son . . . He will be called the Son of God . . . the Holy Spirit will overshadow you .. ."

"I will give birth to the Son of God!" she whispered, her heart profoundly stirred.

She recalled what the angel had told her about Elizabeth. That too was amazing.

"I will go to Elizabeth tomorrow," she decided.

First though, she should tell her parents. And Joseph. He must be told too, but what to tell him? Would he understand? How could she explain? Would he believe her? She would speak to her parents now while the angel's visit was fresh in her mind.

"Mother, father . . . ," she began.

She described the appearance of the angel and related the words he had spoken to her. Her parents listened quietly, and they were as amazed as she had been at the angel's announcement. Her father, they agreed, would tell Joseph. He would possibly wish to break his engagement with her, but that was for him to decide. Mary had told the angel she was God's servant. She must do as He asked.

Mary arose early in the morning and set out on her journey. She longed to see Elizabeth and talk with her.

Elizabeth and her husband Zechariah lived in a small town in Judea. Zechariah was a priest, and they were both godly people, completely devoted to the Lord their God, and committed to keeping His commandments blamelessly. Older by far than Mary, they had no children, so they must be so excited if Elizabeth was in her sixth month!

As soon as Mary entered the house and greeted Elizabeth, her cousin spoke in a loud voice.

"Blessed are you among women, and blessed is the child you will bear! But why am I so favoured, that the mother of my Lord should come to me? As soon as the sound of your greeting reached my ears, the baby in my womb leaped for joy. Blessed is she who has believed that what the Lord has said to her will be accomplished!"

They were exactly the words Mary needed to hear. They were confirmation of what the angel had told her, and she perceived Elizabeth had been given the words by the Holy Spirit. Mary was so overjoyed that she burst into heartfelt words of praise.

"My soul glorifies the Lord and my spirit rejoices in God my Saviour,

For He has been mindful of the humble state of His servant.

From now on all generations will call me blessed,

For the Mighty One has done great things for me—

Holy is His name.

His mercy extends to those who fear Him, from generation to generation.

He has performed mighty deeds with his arm;

He has scattered those who are proud in their inner-most thoughts.

He has brought down rulers from their thrones but has lifted up the humble.

He has filled the hungry with good things but has sent the rich away empty.

He has helped His servant Israel,

Remembering to be merciful to Abraham and his descendants for ever,

Even as he said to our fathers."

Mary stayed with Elizabeth for three months until her cousin's baby was born. All the neighbours and relatives came to rejoice with her because the Lord had shown her such mercy in giving her this child.

The baby was named John, according to the instructions of the angel Gabriel who had appeared to Zechariah before he had come to Mary. Zechariah spoke moving words of prophecy by the Holy Spirit which deeply touched Mary's heart.

"Praise be to the Lord, the God of Israel,

Because He has come and has redeemed His people.

He has raised up a horn of salvation for us in the house of His servant David.

As He said through His holy prophets of long ago,

That we should be saved from our enemies and from the hand of all who hate us,

To perform the mercy promised to our fathers and to remember His holy covenant,

The oath which He swore to our father Abraham:

To grant us that we, being delivered from the hand of our enemies,

Might serve Him without fear, in holiness and righteousness

Before Him all the days of our life."

Listening, Mary realised that Zechariah was speaking of the redemption and salvation that God would bring to His people Israel through the baby who was growing within her. She was a descendant of the house of David, and her son, the Son of the Most High, would be of the house of David as the prophets had foretold centuries ago.

Zechariah then spoke concerning his own son.

"And you my child, will be called a prophet of the Most High;

For you will go on before the Lord to prepare the way for Him,

To give His people the knowledge of salvation through the forgiveness of their sins,

Because of the tender mercy of our God,

By which the rising sun will come to us from heaven

To shine on those living in darkness and in the shadow of death,

To guide our feet into the path of peace."

Richly blessed by her sojourn in the house of her relatives, Mary rejoiced as she journeyed home. They were all descendants of Abraham and Sarah through their son Isaac and their grandson Jacob, later named Israel, who became the father of the twelve tribes, and the Lord had promised great blessings to them as a nation.

Mary recalled words from the prophet Isaiah which she had heard often in the synagogue and also in her home.

"The virgin will be with child and will give birth to a son and will call him Immanuel."

She remembered again the words spoken by the angel Gabriel.

"The holy one to be born of you will be called the Son of God."

"I am the virgin of whom Isaiah spoke!" she whispered reverently.

God would send His son to the earth through her. The words of the prophet would be fulfilled. The child would be called Immanuel, God with us. It was a mystery, but she believed that what God had said would come to pass, and all Israel would be blessed through His coming.

When she arrived home Mary was relieved and happy to hear that Joseph would marry her as planned. An angel of the Lord had appeared to him in a dream.

"Joseph, son of David," the angel had said, "do not be afraid to take Mary home as your wife, because what is conceived in her is from the Holy Spirit. She will give birth to a son, and you are to give him the name Jesus, because he will save his people from their sins."

"I am so glad Joseph knows the truth," Mary said with heartfelt thanksgiving.

Joseph was a good, kind, God-fearing man, and she was grateful that she would have his help, and protection. She would need it in the days that lay ahead.

Chapter 32

yriad stars twinkled in the inky sky, one star shining brighter than all the rest. Mary smiled to herself as she watched it from the bed that Joseph had made for her among the hay, and knew it was a star of special significance.

The night was quiet. No sound could be heard except the gentle breathing of the few oxen with whom they shared the shelter of the stable. It was dark, apart from the gentle glow of light which hovered around the precious baby lying in the manger. The Son of God had been born, and she, blessed above all other women on earth, had given Him birth.

Joseph, his face full of joy and wonder, was leaning over the manger, gazing at the new-born babe lying on the hay, cosily wrapped in swaddling cloths. Suddenly Joseph lifted his head.

"I hear footsteps and voices," he said.

They came hurriedly, excitedly, eager to tell their story, and see the baby in the manger–rough shepherds who had been out in the fields near-by watching over their flocks that night.

Mary sat up, and Joseph greeted them.

"An angel came," the shepherds began. "We were terrified but he told us not to be afraid."

Other shepherds broke in, "The angel said to us, 'Do not be afraid. I bring you good news of great joy that will be for all the people. Today in the town of David a Saviour has been born to you. He is Messiah the Lord. This will be a sign to you: You will find a baby wrapped in swaddling cloths and lying in a manger'".

Joseph beckoned to them, and quickly they huddled around the manger.

"His name is Jesus," Joseph told them softly.

Watching them, it thrilled Mary to see the wonder and adoration on their faces as they beheld the holy child. Some were shedding tears of joy. Others continued the story of their encounter with the angels.

"Suddenly there was a host of angels praising God and saying, 'Glory to God in the highest, and on earth peace to men on whom His favour rests.'"

"As soon as the angels left we said to one another, 'Let us go to Bethlehem and see this thing that has happened, which the Lord has told us about.'"

"And now we have seen Him," said one old shepherd reverently.

"And we will tell everyone about Him," said another.

They could scarcely tear themselves away from the infant Messiah, but finally they left, glorifying and praising God for all the things they had seen and heard.

It was with great joy that Mary had listened to the story the shepherds told. She was so pleased that God had announced the birth of His Son in a spectacular manner. It was fitting that a choir of angels had come from heaven to bring this good news. Her baby was the Saviour, the Messiah, the Son of God.

Another passage from Isaiah came to mind.

"For to us a child is born, to us a son is given, and the government will be upon his shoulders. And he will be called Wonderful Counsellor, Mighty God, Everlasting Father, Prince of Peace."

Only this child, God's Son, could be called by those names.

"What lies ahead for this child?" she wondered.

He would be great, the angel Gabriel had said; He would save His people from their sins. He would be the Son of the Most High. The Lord God would give Him the throne of His father David. What did it all mean?

She was still pondering these questions as she drifted off to sleep.

In the morning others came to see the baby. The shepherds had fulfilled their promise and had told everyone they met.

Kind people offered them room in their house where they could stay until they were able to travel, and Mary and Joseph gratefully accepted. The stable had been of necessity the night before as there was no room in the inn.

"A manger for the Son of God!" thought Mary.

She had not complained, but it had saddened her.

When the baby was eight days old the rite of circumcision was performed on him, and he was formally named Jesus, according to the word of the angel.

"Every firstborn male is to be consecrated to the Lord."

Mary knew the Law of Moses, so this involved a visit to the Temple in Jerusalem where she would offer a sacrifice for her purification after the birth of her son, and where they would present him before the Lord.

As soon as they entered the Temple Mary was surprised to see an old man coming towards them, and even more surprised when he took the child in is arms and began to praise God. She and Joseph marvelled as they listened to him.

"Lord, You are now letting Your servant depart in peace, according to Your word; For my eyes have seen Your salvation which You have prepared before the face of all peoples; a light to bring revelation to the Gentiles, and the glory of Your people Israel."

Mary recognised that Simeon was speaking by the Holy Spirit, and was amazed at what she was hearing. Simeon blessed them and then spoke to her directly.

"This child is destined to cause the falling and rising of many in Israel, and to be a sign that will be spoken against, so that the thoughts of many hearts will be revealed. And a sword will pierce your own soul too."

She had a sudden moment of fear as she wondered what this prophecy might mean. Before she could dwell on it, Anna, an old prophetess who never left the Temple, came in, and coming up to them she too gave thanks for the child.

Mary had much to think about on the journey back to Bethlehem. Little by little she was learning more and more about her special child, and she treasured all these things in her heart.

Chapter 33

usk had gradually turned to dark, and one by one stars were appearing in the night sky. Mary, stepping outside to look up at the starry heavens, noticed with surprise and pleasure that the same bright star which had appeared at Jesus' birth was now shining directly overhead.

"It must mean something," she said to herself.

The mild night air was fragrant with the perfume of blossom, and Mary lingered on, enjoying the stillness of evening, and pondering the meaning of the bright star's reappearance.

Presently, the sound of hooves on the ground caused her heart to beat a little faster. Perhaps the reason for the star was about to be revealed. Joseph came to the door to see who was coming.

As they came closer, Mary could see men on camels, and noticed that they were gazing upwards at the star, seemingly overjoyed to see it. Joseph stepped forward to greet them as they dismounted.

"We have come to see the newborn king," they announced. "We have seen his star in the east and have come to worship him."

They were rich men, judging by their clothing and jewels. Mary wondered from what country they had come as Joseph led them inside. She lifted the baby and held him on her lap so that the visitors could see him. When they saw the child they immediately bowed down before him. Watching them Mary could see the same joy and wonder on their faces that she had seen on the shepherd's faces. They opened up their treasures and presented him with gifts of gold, frankincense and myrrh.

"Strange gifts," thought Mary. "What do they mean?"

As they talked the men revealed that they were eastern kings of small states who were also Magi with an interest in the stars. They explained that when they first saw the star they concluded that it indicated the birth of a new king, a Jewish king, so accordingly they travelled to Jerusalem believing it to be the most likely place to find a new Jewish king. They had arrived at Herod's palace asking, "Where is he who has been born king of the Jews?"

"King Herod sent us to Bethlehem," said one, "after he had consulted the chief priests and teachers of the Law."

"They read from the prophet Micah," said another.

Mary listened attentively as the eastern Magi quoted the prophet.

"But you Bethlehem, in the land of Judah, are not the least among the rulers of Judah; For out of you shall come a Ruler who will shepherd My people Israel."

Mary had heard it before, but hearing it now she understood why she had had to come to Bethlehem. The infant Jesus was descended from King David through her, so it was appropriate that he should be born in Bethlehem, the city of David. Even the decree of the Roman governor, that everyone must return to their city of origin so that a census could be taken, made sense now. Joseph and she were both descendants of David, Joseph through Solomon and she through Nathan, both of them sons of David and Bathsheba.

God, who had inspired Micah to make this prophecy, had ensured that His Son would be born in Bethlehem through the issuing of this decree.

Mary listened with interest as the Magi brought their story to an end.

"King Herod told us to go and make a careful search for the child," they concluded. "He said, 'As soon as you find him, report to me so that I too may go and worship him.'"

After the visitors had gone Mary and Joseph talked it over. It had been another extraordinary encounter with worshippers sent by God through a sign: the heavenly choir of angels had brought the shepherds, and the bright new star had led the eastern kings to Bethlehem. Mary pondered it all as she lay down to sleep.

She awakened some time later with Joseph gently nudging her arm as he leaned over her.

"Mary, we must leave at once. I have had a dream . An angel spoke to me."

Mary gasped.

Joseph continued, "The angel said, 'Arise, take the young child and his mother, flee to Egypt, and stay there until I bring you word; for Herod will seek the young child to destroy him.'"

Hastily they gathered together their few belongings, wrapped the baby snuggly, and left in the dead of night. Even as they departed Mary knew that Herod would waste no time in seeking her precious child, not to worship him, but to kill him.

They reached Egypt after weary days of travel, but they were safe. Mary knew that God was watching over His Son.

Chapter 34

" ehold the Lamb of God who takes away the sin of the world."

They were the prophetic words of Elizabeth's son John when he saw Jesus coming towards him. Mary heard them from others who had been there, and the prophecy of Zechariah, John's father, reverberated in her heart.

"And you, my child, will be called a prophet of the Most High; for you will go on before the Lord to prepare the way for Him."

Six months older than Jesus, John was fulfilling his mission, calling people to repentance for their sins, and baptising them in the River Jordan. Some people wondered if John was the promised Messiah, but John quickly enlightened them.

"I am not the Messiah," he told them.

"Who are you then?" he was asked.

"I am the voice of one crying in the desert, 'Make straight the way for the Lord.'"

Mary found her thoughts turning constantly to her firstborn son. More and more it was becoming clear to others as well that he was the Son of God. John had shown both his own purpose and that of Jesus when he answered those who came asking questions of him.

"I myself did not know him, but the reason I came baptising with water was that he might be revealed to Israel."

Jesus had come to him for baptism, not because he needed to repent, but to fulfil God's purposes. John afterwards testified concerning the experience.

"I saw the Spirit come down from heaven as a dove and remain on him. I would not have known him, except that the One who sent me to baptise with water told me, 'The man on whom you see the Spirit come down and remain is he who will baptise with the Holy Spirit.' I have seen and I testify that this is the Son of God."

It moved Mary to tears. Once again, as she had so many times before, she felt so privileged to be the mother of the Son of God.

"How quickly the years have gone by!" she mused.

The sweet days of his babyhood and the happy days of his childhood had gone. He was now thirty years old, the age of maturity for a young man, and he had left to follow the path laid out for him. She had always known that he had a divine purpose to fulfil on the earth, but as she watched him go she knew she would miss him greatly.

The years had been good years. They had returned to Nazareth, their home town, after the Lord had appeared to Joseph in a dream, telling him to return to the land of Israel, for those who sought the child's life were dead. Jesus had helped Joseph in his carpenter's shop, and he had helped her with his younger brothers and sisters.

"Yes, they were good years," Mary acknowledged. "Now it is time for him to be about his Father's business, as he said himself when he was twelve years old."

Jesus had been away for a few weeks, but word was spreading quickly that he was returning to Nazareth. She hoped he would come in time for the Sabbath.

As was customary the family attended the syna-gogue on the Sabbath, and it was no surprise to Mary when Jesus stood up to read. Silently he took the scroll that was handed to him, and as he began to read every eye was on him.

"The Spirit of the Lord is upon me, because He has anointed me to preach the gospel to the poor; He has sent me to heal the broken-hearted, to proclaim liberty to the captives and recovery of sight to the blind, to set at liberty those who are oppressed; to proclaim the acceptable year of the Lord."

When he had finished reading from the prophet Isaiah he spoke to the waiting group of worshippers.

"Today this Scripture is fulfilled in your hearing."

Mary's eyes filled with sudden tears. So many times since he had been born, and even before his birth, she had seen the prophecies of Isaiah fulfilled. This was another.

At first she was pleased to see that the townsfolk of Nazareth thought well of him. She could hear their comments all around her.

"Where did this man get these things?"

"What is this wisdom that has been given him, that he even does miracles!"

But others said, "Is this not the carpenter? Is this not Mary's son and the brother of James, Joseph, Judas and Simon? Are not his sisters here with us?"

Sadly they did not accept that he was more than a carpenter, more than just Mary's son, and they quickly turned against him because they were offended by the way he preached, so they drove him away. Mary understood that he had to leave. She knew that he went to Capernaum, and there he chose a group of twelve men who became known as his disciples. She was glad he had these companions around him so that he was not alone. She looked forward to meeting them soon at a family wedding in Cana, but meantime she was glad to hear of all he was doing; healing the sick, giving sight to the blind, preaching and teaching.

The day of the wedding came, and it was a joyful occasion. Everybody was there; Jesus and his twelve disciples, and the whole family as well as other wedding guests. Mary was enjoying herself, especially being able to spend time with Jesus again, when she became aware that the wine had run out! This was embarrassing at a wedding!

She would speak to Jesus. He would help, she was sure.

"They have no more wine," she told him.

"Dear woman," he replied, "Why do you involve me? My time has not yet come."

She stood silently for a moment, puzzled by what he had said.

"What did I expect him to do?" she asked herself.

The answer came immediately. A miracle! Had he been testing her to see if she believed in him? She smiled. Was it not time to reveal to others his true identity?

Turning to the servants she said confidently, "Do whatever he tells you."

Nearby stood six large stone jars which usually held water for ceremonial cleansing.

Jesus said to the servants, "Fill the jars with water."

Mary watched as the servants filled them up to the brim.

Jesus turned to them again and said, "Now draw some out and take it to the master of the banquet."

It was a joy to watch as the master sampled the wine, and Mary could tell by the expression on his face that he was pleased with the taste. Moving closer to listen to what he was saying to the bridegroom she was delighted with what she heard.

"Every man at the beginning sets out the good wine, and when the guests have drunk well, then the inferior, but you have kept the good wine until now."

It was a defining moment. Jesus had revealed his glory. Tears of gladness filled Mary's eyes, and the disciples of Jesus gathered around him with happy faces. They too had seen his glory and they looked at him with new eyes. They experienced their first glimmer of understanding that this man they followed was no ordinary man. The miracle he had performed came from the realm of heaven.

There was a tangible sense of joy in the room, Mary realised. The bride and groom, the disciples and the guests had all been blessed by the presence of the Son of God. They would remember this day always, for the abundance of joy it brought to a family wedding in the little town of Cana in Galilee.

Chapter 35

The knock on the door sounded urgent and Mary hurried to answer it. A young boy stood there panting and out of breath. It was clear he had come in a hurry.

"They have arrested Jesus," he burst out.

Mary stared at him wide-eyed before she found her voice.

"Why?" was all she could ask..

"I do not know," stammered the boy. "I was just sent to tell you."

Mary leaned against the wall for support. She felt faint. Other family members rushed to her side, shocked too by this news. They had all come to Jerusalem for the Passover Feast and were staying with relatives in the city, but they had not expected this to happen.

"Where have they taken him? Why has this happened? Oh, how can this be?"

Later, word came that Jesus had been taken to the High priest to be questioned, but it was too late to try to see him that night. They would have to wait until morning.

Greatly distressed, Mary paced up and down thinking deeply. She knew that many people believed in Jesus as he had gone up and down the country over the last three years, preaching, teaching and healing all manner of sickness and disease. He had done such good! But he had enemies too. The Pharisees and chief rulers hated him because he had shown them up for the hypocrites they were. They were always trying to trip him up, constantly finding fault and picking arguments with him. He had shaken the very foundations of their religious beliefs and they did not like it.

"What are they doing with him now?" she wondered.

She had no doubt the chief priests were behind his arrest, so he would be at their mercy. She could not imagine they would show him any compassion. What would happen to him?

Mary slept little, so she was awake when her friends came to the house early in the morning. They had heard of the arrest and came with news that the Chief Priest had sent him to Pilate, the Roman Governor. This was not good news.

Noisy crowds thronged the city, and as Mary and her friends joined them they were pushed and jostled along with everybody else. All around them people were talking excitedly, some shouting, others speaking in subdued tones, many women weeping.

"They are taking him away to be crucified," Mary heard.

Her legs gave way under her. Were they speaking of Jesus?

"No, no, not Jesus, not my son, not the Son of God," her heart cried, but she could speak no words.

Her sister-in-law and another woman friend came alongside her, and taking her arms they supported her as they followed the crowd. Ahead was a detachment of soldiers who were escorting their prisoners to their execution. Was Jesus among them?

Mary and her friends surged forward, and then suddenly, through a gap in the crowd, they saw Jesus. Mary swooned as she caught sight of him. His back was torn and bleeding, and his face, his face . . . ! Sobs wracked

Mary's body as she looked at him. Someone, probably the soldiers, had pressed a crown of thorns on his head and he was bleeding profusely. She could not bear to see her son's beloved face so marred and distorted with pain. How could they do this to him? She moaned and turned away.

Stumbling under the weight of the heavy wooden cross he was forced to carry, he could scarcely take the next step. Finally, the soldiers, impatient to get to the place of crucifixion, pulled a man out of the crowd and made him carry the cross.

At last they reached Golgotha, a rocky outcrop on the edge of the city, just outside the walls. Mary could scarcely bear to look as the soldiers forced each prisoner to lie on his cross with his arms outstretched. Again she cried out in anguish. She did not want to witness what was happening but she felt compelled to be with her son to share in his sufferings, yet his were so much greater than hers.

"All you who pass by, behold and see if there is any sorrow like my sorrow."

Words from one of the prophets struck her, and she knew with certainty they were meant for this time. At this moment she recalled also Simeon's words in the Temple.

"A sword shall pierce your own soul."

Every blow of the hammer, as the soldiers nailed him to the cross, felt like a sword being twisted in her heart.

The soldiers raised the crosses and hammered them into the ground. A sign above the cross of Jesus read, "This is Jesus, the King of the Jews." The crowd sat down to watch, some to scoff, others to weep. Mary and her friends stood at a short distance. John came to stand beside them, but none of his other disciples were in sight. Other women were there, friends of Jesus who cared for him; Mary Magdalene, Salome, the mother of James and John, Joanna and others. All were deeply shocked and saddened. They had not expected this. They, like Mary, could barely take it in.

Nailed to a cross! Why? Mary knew it was the harsh Roman method of execution for criminals, but Jesus was not a criminal. He had done nothing to deserve this.

"How could God let this happen? He was God's perfect, sinless Son. Why?"

The thoughts that rushed through her mind seemingly had no answer.

Her friends and John stood close to her, supporting her. There was nothing any of them could do but stay near him and watch.

Jesus was speaking from the cross.

"Father, forgive them, for they do not know what they are doing."

He could forgive them!

Then the anguished cry, "My God, my God, why have you forsaken me."

It tore at Mary's heart. That it came from one of King David's poems, she knew. He had written it centuries ago. How could he have known?

At the foot of the cross the soldiers were gambling for his clothes. Hardened to these crucifixions, what did they care?

The chief priests and rulers who had called for his death were scoffing and sneering. They too cared nothing. This was what they had wanted for a long time.

"He saved others; let him save himself if he is the Messiah of God, the chosen One," they shouted scathingly.

The soldiers too took up the mocking cry.

"If you are the king of the Jews, save yourself."

One of the criminals also began to hurl insults at him. "Are you not the Messiah? Save yourself and us."

But strangely, the other criminal intervened in his defence.

"Do you not fear God," he said, "since you are under the same sentence? We are punished justly, for we are getting what our deeds deserve. But this man has done nothing wrong."

It provided one brief glimpse of light in the darkness of Mary's heart.

"Jesus, remember me when you come into your kingdom" the repentant one asked.

Turning to him Jesus said, "I tell you the truth, today you will be with me in paradise."

The words were a balm to Mary's soul in the midst of her anguish. He would soon be with his Father.

Suddenly the sun disappeared behind heavy clouds, and darkness came over the whole land. It seemed fitting.

"This must be the darkest day the world has ever known," Mary thought.

Then Jesus was speaking to her. She could scarcely bear to look at him, so pitiful was the sight of her lovely son, bruised and bleeding from head and hands and feet.

"Dear woman," he said. "Here is your son."

And to John, "Here is your mother."

He had thought of her in the midst of all his agony. She turned her head into John's chest and sobbed.

Together they watched. He could not last out much longer, Mary thought. Blood was pouring from his body, soaking the ground beneath the cross. His breathing was shallow, coming in short spurts. Oh that it would stop and end his torment!

"I am thirsty," he said.

A sponge was soaked in wine vinegar and reached up to him. When he took it he spoke again in a loud voice.

"It is finished!"

In spite of his pain it was a cry of triumph. With that, Jesus bowed his head and spoke once more, his voice strangely strong.

"Father, into Your hands I commit my spirit."

Mary watched sorrowfully as he breathed his last. He was gone. Now she could let her tears flow freely.

His agony was over and he had gone back to his Father. But without him life would never be the same again.

They did not hurry away. John and she and the other women who were there huddled together in a little group, shocked beyond belief by the terrible happenings, heart-broken over the One who had meant so much to all of them. Quietly they stood together, unwilling to leave, yet knowing there was nothing more they could do. As they lingered the soldiers returned and in a final act, pierced his side with a sword.

Mary did not know how long they waited, but at length two men approached the cross, dignified -looking men. John knew them: Nicodemus, who had once talked with Jesus, and Joseph of Arimathea, both members of the Sanhedrin. They had asked Pilate for the body of Jesus, and now they gently took his body down, wrapped it in strips of linen along with the spices they had brought, carried him carefully to a new tomb in a near-by garden and placed him there. Then they sealed the entrance with a large, heavy stone.

Satisfied that his body had been given a dignified burial, and knowing that the Sabbath was near, Mary,

John and the other women left that dreadful place of suffering and went home.

Chapter 36

*I*t was the third day since Jesus had died. Mary slept late, having had little sleep the previous few nights. Today she felt calmer, and more rested, but still so sad.

John had gone out, but he had been so kind to her. Yesterday, on the Sabbath, he had talked quietly most of the day about Jesus, the Master, as he called him.

"'Do not let your heart be troubled' he told us. 'Trust in God; trust also in me. In my Father's house are many rooms. I am going there to prepare a place for you. And if I go and prepare a place for you, I will come back and take you to be with me, that you also may be where I am.'"

Mary was not sure what they meant, but they were such comforting words!

John remembered many things. He told her about the time Nicodemus had come to Jesus, secretly at night time, and Jesus had told him, "God so loved the world that He gave His one and only Son, that whoever believes in him shall not perish but have eternal life."

Then there was the feeding of five thousand people with five small loaves and two fish.

Afterwards Jesus had told them, "I am the bread of life. He who comes to me shall never hunger, and he who believes in me shall never thirst."

"And there was the wedding in Cana where he turned the water into wine." Mary said. She smiled at the memory. It had been such a joyous occasion.

"And there was the raising of Lazarus from the dead," John said softly. "Jesus wept when he went to Martha and Mary. He said to Martha, 'I am the resurrection and the life. He who believes in me, though he may die, he shall live. And whoever lives and believes in me shall never die.'"

They became silent, lost in contemplation of these amazing words, not fully comprehending them.

John spoke again. "He made blind people see, lame people walk, deaf people hear. He was a master story-teller. He used simple illustrations from everyday life."

Mary waited as John sat deep in thought. Then he resumed.

"He likened us to sheep in a sheepfold. He said, 'I am the gate; whoever enters through me will be saved. He will come in and go out, and find pasture.'"

"Like David's poem about the shepherd giving us green pastures," thought Mary.

John paused for a moment, thinking, then he went on, "Jesus said, 'I am the good shepherd. The good shepherd lays down his life for the sheep.'"

Again they both sat quietly, meditating on these words.

"On the evening of his arrest, while he was still with us, Jesus said, 'Love each other as I have loved you. Greater love has no-one than this, that he lay down his life for his friends.'"

They both became silent again. He *had* given his life.

Mary sat quietly thinking over all these things. There had been many thoughts she had kept hidden deep in her heart through the years. Now there were new ones. John had given her much to think about. She was still pondering them when John came in. He was smiling softly, and looking at him Mary detected a far-away look in his eyes as if he had discovered a secret joy but was not yet ready to reveal it.

"Mary Magdalene came to Peter and me early this morning," he began. "She told us that she had gone to the tomb, and that the stone had been taken away."

Mary felt a pang of dismay.

John continued, "Peter and I went to the tomb, and we saw that the grave clothes were folded neatly, but Jesus was not there. I believe . . . "

Just then Mary Magdalene rushed in, her face radiant.

"I have seen the Lord!" she burst out.

All eyes were on her as she told her story.

"I went to the tomb and found that the stone had been taken away. I went inside and saw two angels, but Jesus was not there."

While Mary was still speaking other women came crowding into the house, full of excitement, bursting to tell what they had seen. They could scarcely contain themselves while Mary finished her account.

Mary Magdalene continued, her eyes glowing. "There was a man outside the tomb but at first I did not know who he was. Then as soon as he spoke my name I knew he was Jesus, and I fell at his feet. He said 'Do not cling to me, for I have not yet ascended to my Father; but go to my brothers and say to them, 'I am ascending to my Father and your Father, and to my God and your God.'"

At this the other women broke in, "We have seen him too! We saw the angels first and they said to us, 'Do not be afraid, for I know that you seek Jesus who was crucified. He is not here; for he has risen as he said. Come, see the place where the Lord lay.

"Then they told us, 'Go quickly and tell his disciples that he has risen from the dead, and he is going before you into Galilee; there you will see him.'

"As we were going we met him, and he spoke to us and said, 'Rejoice!' And he told us to tell his disciples to go to Galilee where they would see him. We told them but they did not believe us."

"I believe you," said John quietly. "I believed when I saw the empty tomb."

There were tears in every eye The Lord had risen! There could be no better news!

As they went out to tell the others, Mary lingered behind. She needed a quiet moment to reflect. Overwhelming peace and joy filled her heart. Her beloved son, God's Son, was alive! Profound thankfulness washed over her. He had died at the hands of wicked men, but God raised him from the dead. She recalled another of her ancestor David's poems, written long ago, inspired by God's Holy Spirit.

"You will not leave my soul in Sheol, nor allow Your Holy One to see corruption."

Mary's thoughts moved forward to the present again. He had appeared to Mary Magdalene and the other women. Would he come to her?

Suddenly he was there, a gentle smile on his beloved face.

"Son!"

They had precious time together. Her heart sang with happiness such as she had never known before. Another lovely phrase from David's poem came to her.

"In your presence is fullness of joy; at your right hand are pleasures forevermore!"

Her cup of happiness was full!

Chapter 37

*I*t had been the most amazing and wonderful day! A day of rapturous joy and deep heart-gladness! If the day Jesus died had been the darkest on earth, this was the most joyous the world had ever known. He was alive, and they had seen him!

Tonight Mary could not sleep for sheer happiness. John had come in late, and he had so much to tell her. After they had heard from the women that Jesus was alive, the disciples gathered together with the doors locked, still fearful of the Jewish authorities.

"Jesus came and stood among us," John told her in an awed voice.

John's voice almost broke with emotion as he talked.

"He showed us his hands and his side, and again he said, 'Peace be with you. As the Father has sent me, I am sending you.'"

Mary listened avidly.. She wanted to hear everything.

John went on, "Some of us could scarcely believe it was really he who was standing there with us, but when he asked us for some food, we gave him a piece of broiled fish and he ate it in our presence."

"Then Jesus said, 'This is what I told you while I was still with you: Everything must be fulfilled that is written about me in the Law of Moses, the Prophets and the Psalms.'"

His words resonated in Mary's heart. She had so often recognised passages in the Scriptures concerning him.

John continued. "He opened up our minds so that we could understand the Scriptures. He told us, 'This is what is written: The Messiah will suffer and rise from the dead on the third day, and repentance and forgiveness of sins will be preached in his name to all nations, beginning at Jerusalem. You are witnesses of these things. I am going to send you what my Father promised; but stay in the city until you have been endued with power from on high.'"

"What had his father promised?" wondered Mary.

"The Holy Spirit,." said John quietly.

After John left, Mary still sat meditating. She understood so much more now. She let her thoughts wander back over the years.

The angel Gabriel was the first to speak of Jesus. "He will be called the Son of the Most High." he had told her.

At the time of John's birth, Zechariah had spoken by the Holy Spirit, "The Lord has come and has redeemed His people; He has raised up a horn of salvation for us in the house of His servant David."

Joseph, her husband, had been told by the angel, "You are to give him the name Jesus because he will save his people from their sins."

The shepherds had been given the good news, "Today in the town of David a Saviour has been born to you; He is Messiah the Lord."

Magi from the east had come seeking one who had been born king of the Jews.

Simeon in the Temple had declared , "My eyes have seen your salvation, which you have prepared in the sight of all people."

Mary had accepted all these marvellous statements without question, but what she had not understood three days ago was why the Son of God had to die. None of them had understood, neither his disciples, nor his friends and loved ones. Now she recalled passages of Scripture which explained it.

"It was the Lord's will to crush him and cause him to suffer," Isaiah had written.

"Why?" she had wondered at first, but as she meditated, it became clear to her.

"Because he poured out his life unto death, and was numbered with the transgressors. For he bore the sins of many."

She and John had talked about it. He had given his life willingly to save his people from their sins. She thought of what Elizabeth's son John had said, and was suddenly enlightened. When he saw Jesus coming towards him he said, "Behold the Lamb of God who takes away the sin of the world."

Jesus was, as it were, the sacrificial lamb. Just as the people of Israel brought a lamb as a sacrifice for their sins, so God gave His Son as the sacrificial Lamb for the sins of His people. "God so loved the world," Jesus said, "that He gave His Son."

John had just told her what Jesus had said to his disciples this very evening.

"Repentance and forgiveness of sins will be preached in his name to all nations, beginning in Jerusalem."

The whole world was to hear about the Saviour through the disciples. It was exciting.

Mary's reminiscences deepened. What had God said to Abraham centuries ago?

"All peoples on earth will be blessed through you."

It was amazing to think that away back then in Abraham's time, God was planning to bless the whole world through a descendant of Abraham and Sarah. From their family tree had eventually come David, from David and Bathsheba had come Nathan who was her own ancestor, and through her, Jesus, the Saviour, had been born.

Mary paused in her reasoning, another thought occurring to her. Even before Abraham's time, God had made a statement that Eve took as a promise.

"I will put enmity between you and the woman, and between your offspring and hers; he will crush your head, and you will strike his heel."

Who was the woman's offspring who would crush the head of the serpent? Not Eve's sons. David? He was the ruler of Israel in his time, but he had not crushed the Evil One. It suddenly dawned on her. As perfectly as a candle lights up a dark room, a light was lit in Mary's soul.

Jesus had broken Satan's power because he had brought forgiveness of sins to all who believed on him. Satan was the one who had brought the curse of sin into the world in the beginning by corrupting Adam and Eve. Now the world was no longer under that curse because it had been broken by the Son of God. He had crushed the serpent's head through his own suffering and death as the Saviour. Now he had risen, showing that he was victorious over death which had come through the curse.

That is why he told Martha, "I am the resurrection and the life. He who believes in me will live, even though he dies; and whoever lives and believes in me will never die."

Mary understood. They would live with him in heaven eternally, even though they would die physically. Again she thanked God for the privilege of being the mother of the Saviour. He was God's divine Son but he had chosen to live and die as a human.

As she laid her head down to sleep, she had one more amazing thought. Her offspring had crushed the serpent! That made her the Woman of The Promise!

Chapter 38

They were all together in one place; waiting, united, expectant. The company was made up of Mary and her family, the disciples and many others, both men and women, who were waiting for the promised Holy Spirit.

Jesus had gone back to heaven, but before his departure he had met often with his disciples to teach them and prepare them for the work they were to do in the world.

"You will be baptised with the Holy Spirit not many days from now," he told them.

"Lord, are you at this time going to restore the kingdom to Israel?" they had asked.

It was a natural question. Under the Roman occupation it was the desire of every Jew to gain control of their own land again, and they had hoped that Jesus, as Messiah, would be their deliverer, but clearly, it was not to be at this time.

"It is not for you to know the times or dates the Father has set by His own authority," He told them. "But you will receive power when the Holy Spirit comes on you; and you will be my witnesses in Jerusalem, and in all Judea and Samaria, and to the ends of the earth."

The disciples related all these things to Mary and the other believers, about one hundred and twenty of them, all of whom had seen Jesus since His resurrection. In an upper room in Jerusalem where the disciples stayed while they were in the city, they all met daily to listen and to pray.

It would only be when they had received the Holy Spirit that they would be enabled to fulfil their commission to bring the good news of forgiveness and eternal life to the people of Israel, and even beyond to the ends of the earth.

Mary recalled yet another prophecy from Isaiah. It too would be fulfilled.

"A light to lighten the Gentiles, and the glory of My people Israel."

After Jesus had commissioned them and told them to wait for the coming of the Holy Spirit, the disciples saw Him being taken up to heaven before their very eyes, a cloud covering him as He ascended. They described it to the eager listeners.

"As we were looking up intently into the sky as He was going, two men dressed in white appeared to us.

'Men of Galilee,' the angels said, Why do you stand here looking into the sky? This same Jesus, who has been taken from you into heaven, will come back in the same way you have seen Him go into heaven.'"

To Mary, this illuminated another of the sayings of Jesus: "I will come back again and take you to be where I am."

So now they knew He would come back in the same spectacular manner, even though they did not know when that would be. It was something to look forward to. Meantime they were to wait.

Mary had experienced the Holy Spirit earlier in her life, through Elizabeth, Zechariah, and Simeon. She herself had spoken words of praise by the power of the Spirit. This would be different though. It would be the coming of the Holy Spirit into the world to all believers, sent from God the Father at the behest of Jesus the Son.

"I will ask the Father," Jesus had said, "and He will give you another Counsellor to be with you forever–the Spirit of truth."

As they prayed in the quietness of the upper room, suddenly everything changed. They heard "a sound from heaven like a rushing, mighty wind, which filled the whole house where they were sitting, and they saw what appeared to be tongues of fire which came and sat upon each of them. They were all filled with the Holy Spirit and began to speak in other languages as the Spirit enabled them." At once they went out into the streets, praising and glorifying God and declaring His wonders to the people who had come from far and near to Jerusalem for the Feast.

Peter, now the accepted leader of the twelve disciples, stood up before them all and explained what was happening.

"This is what was spoken by the prophet Joel: 'In the last days, God says, I will pour out my Spirit on all people . . . . Even on My servants, both men and women, I will pour out My Spirit in those days, and they will prophecy.'"

Peter preached powerfully and with great passion. He outlined all that had happened to Jesus from the time He was arrested, put to death and raised again from the dead by God, declaring, "God has made this Jesus, whom you crucified, both Lord and Messiah."

To those who took it to heart Peter said, "Repent and be baptised, every one of you, in the name of the Messiah, Jesus for the forgiveness of your sins. And you will receive the gift of the Holy Spirit. The promise is for you and your children and for all who are far off– for all whom the Lord our God will call."

Many were convicted by Peter's sermon through the power of the Spirit, and by the end of the day three thousand souls had repented and believed.

Mary's heart was full. As she thought again of the life, death, resurrection and ascension of Jesus she realised afresh how privileged she had been to give Him birth and care for Him throughout His childhood. There were times she had almost forgotten He was God's Son, but she had always known that He had come to fulfil God's plan and purpose on earth. He had accomplished all that His Father had sent Him to do, and now He had fulfilled his promise to send His Spirit who would be with her always.

"I will come back and take you to be with me that you also may be where I am."

Such beautiful comforting words! No-one knew when, but He would come back. He had promised and He would keep His promises.

Meanwhile she, the woman of the Promise, would love and trust the Son of the Promise, as she waited for His glorious return! And if her life on earth ended before then, so be it. She would go to be with Him in heaven forever.

Lightning Source UK Ltd.
Milton Keynes UK
UKOW07f0606231114

242026UK00001B/6/P